DANCING
IN THE HEART
OF THE
DRAGON

Wash Your Heart

DANCING IN THE HEART OF THE DRAGON

A Memoir of China

Xīn xiǎng shì chéng

May the dreams of your
heart come true

Ramona McKean

Ramona McKean

First Published in Canada 2013 by Influence Publishing

Book cover design: Nicholas Jones
Author photo: Melanie Alsdorf
All other photos: Provided by author

DISCLAIMER: This book is a work of Non-Fiction. Some of the names of characters in this book have been changed to protect their privacy.

Dedication

To the Essence uniting all that is,
and to people the world over who
awaken to its presence and respond to its call.

Acknowledgements

Several people, either directly or indirectly, have helped to support my writing of this book.

I wish to thank all the people in China and Canada who helped me survive then recover from a serious accident, friends and family members too numerous to mention. Without them, there would be no story. Words cannot adequately express the depth of my appreciation for all their love and amazing support. To friends I have made since my recovery, I say thank you as well, for listening to me and believing I can do what I set out to do.

When Julie Salisbury, owner of Influence Publishing, said "yes" to my story, my inner knowing said "yes" too. (The best sign for me.) Her expertise and purpose inspired my trust. Her enthusiasm uplifted me, and her direction grounded me. For all, I am grateful.

I appreciate the editorial support of three remarkable women, dedicated to providing excellent service. Caroline Mufford, Esther Hart and Sally Jennings all helped me at varying stages of this book. For their clear-sightedness combined with timely flexibility, I say thank you.

The friendly, cooperative manner of Greg Salisbury, Production Manager, made him a pleasure to work with. I also appreciate the extensive knowledge he brought to solving problems I faced.

I am most grateful to Dré Lavack for technological support.

Nicholas Jones, my cover artist, I thank for his bold creativity.

Individuals in many countries have taught me much about Chinese culture through music posted on Youtube. I give special thanks to GeorgeForTeresaTeng1, wwwtips, Teisuka and Baohuluxiake.

Sometimes an invisible hand directs the course of my meeting certain other people. The instant rapport and same eagerness to share, learn and help each other is abundantly apparent virtually right away. Such was my experience with the remaining people I wish to acknowledge. "*You yuan*"—we were meant to meet. "Invisible Hand," you're awesome!

One day my daughter happened to say hello to a Chinese couple with their little girl at a dock in Sooke, British Columbia. She said, "Maybe you'd like to meet my mom. She's writing a book on some of her experiences in China and I know she'd love to meet you." Li Huihui and Liu Hang from the Northwestern Polytechnical University in Xian, China, were indeed a joy to meet. A geologist and a computer scientist, they were in the middle of their one year tenure at the University of Victoria as visiting professors. We met many times during their remaining months in Canada. Our cross-cultural exchanges were enjoyable, fascinating and rewarding. They helped me enormously with the thousand and one questions I had on Chinese culture and history. Of course, it was my pleasure to answer their many questions on life as I knew it as a Westerner. I look forward to visiting them the next time I venture to China.

Meng Xin in New York City I met online through youtube, where he posts videos by many wonderful artists, including Deng Lijun. In no time, after my commenting on his videos, we were online friends, corresponding about my book; then I was able to meet him and his family in New York City. Xin has provided me with much encouragement and a deeper understanding of Chinese cultural matters. For his friendship and support I am most grateful.

When I first heard of Sidney and Yulin Rittenberg in early 2007, I knew I had to meet them, especially given Sidney's advancing years. I managed to contact them at their home in Washington State and readily discovered their kindness and generosity. Sidney sent me a personalized copy of his book *The Man Who Stayed Behind* and invited me to visit them. An American leading force in China from the early days of Communism, Sidney was imprisoned twice, for a total of 16 years. Both times he was in solitary confinement. His wife and children did not abandon him. For Sidney and Yulin's courage, strength and exceptional good-heartedness, I am deeply grateful. For their vision of a world united, I am inspired.

And last, but really first, I express gratitude to Essence, *God*, whose presence when I am awake to it makes all the difference. For the depth of my thankfulness, there are no words.

Testimonials

Ramona Mckean, in Dancing in the Heart of the Dragon, makes a truly great and important statement, not just about China but about the human race. She understands that our grandchildren's future depends largely on understanding between Chinese and Westerners. Her gripping story powerfully reveals why and how this understanding is possible. The outlook on life, the philosophy is tremendous, shared with simple, direct, honest eloquence, no tricks, no holds barred, no preaching. When all is said and done, at the end of the day it's about having a good heart. Ramona has a good heart. I am proud to support her story.
Sidney Rittenberg, author of *The Man Who Stayed Behind,* journalist, scholar, Chinese linguist, Professor of China Studies at Pacific Lutheran University, and subject of the documentary *The Revolutionary*

A good memoir is a glimpse into a soul. Ramona McKean has given us more than a glimpse in Dancing in the Heart of the Dragon. She lays bare her tragic experience in China that almost cost her life. Through journal and recollection, she allows us to follow her journey through a new door to an amazing future.
John Shields, author of *The Priest Who Left His Religion - In Pursuit of Cosmic Spirituality*

Rarely does a book come along that changes the way I view the world. Dancing in the Heart of the Dragon is one of those books. This miraculous true story of survival from a head-on crash in China inspires me with hope for healing on a global scale. I felt like I was taken into Ramona's own heart and mind when she touchingly portrayed the people she met in China, especially her caregivers. I felt like my heart and mind were

united also with theirs. Through her experiences, Ramona McKean has helped me both to understand China better and to see China in a new and more respectful light. This is a good thing when I consider China's growing influence. I feel a new spirit of friendship for our big neighbour across the sea. Perhaps you'll feel the same when you read Ramona's timely and inspirational story.
Bobby O'Neal (aka. Dr Love), author of *Dr. Love's Prescription for a Romantic Loving Man*, and creator of *Syncrohearts Board Game*

Ramona is a brilliant story teller with a remarkable story - a true hero's journey. Make sure you don't start reading at bedtime or you will be up all night! A powerful story of one woman, two countries and a heart that learns to embrace both.
Junie Swadron, author of *Re-Write Your Life*

In Dancing in the Heart of the Dragon, Ramona McKean focuses on her friendships with members of the new generation of Chinese, the transitional generation, who help her to understand China's culture through idioms. Surviving a tragic accident also gives her a unique perspective that enables her to touch contemporary China's pulse closer than many other Western writers. I believe that Ramona knows the problems the Chinese government and society are facing, and she believes that pointing a finger at China is not going to make things better. A positive approach with new understanding will help to solve present problems. Dancing in the Heart of the Dragon is a story of courage, inspiration and that new kind of understanding.
Kefen Zhou, author, journalist, translator, former editor of the Shenzhen Economic Daily and former instructor of Chinese literature at the University of Victoria

Ramona McKean and I have been friends since meeting in Harbin in 2004. When I hold her book *Dancing in the Heart of the Dragon* in my hands I feel deeply moved, as I know how much love and effort she put into writing it. Although Ramona had a terrible accident in China, what I see in her book is not hatred nor complaints, but love for her students and for the people she met, also an eagerness to share, to learn about China and to bridge misunderstanding between our different cultures. I also see how much work we Chinese people need to do with, for instance, our health care system, emergency response and environmental education so that we can catch up with the developed world in ways not only technological. In Ramona's book I have found a wise, caring and beautiful soul rising from the flames of a deadly accident. I am inspired and encouraged to pass her love, care and understanding on.

Songhe Wang, PhD, linguistics professor, Heilongjiang University, Harbin, China

Table of Contents

Dedication

Acknowledgements

Testimonials

Table of Contents

Map

Prologue 1

Section One: The Miracle of Getting Home 5

Section Two: Earlier 19

Section Three: Recovery 43

Section Four: Introducing My Young Friends 55

Section Five: Communication from China 63

Section Six: Back to a Time of Happiness 69

Section Seven: Three Handsome Dudes 85

Section Eight: The In-Between Time 101

Section Nine: Back in Canada 135

Section Ten: Insult Added to Injury 153

Section Eleven: Love Affair with a Nation 167

Epilogue 187

Glossary of Chinese Terms 191

Book Club Discussions 197

Author Biography 201

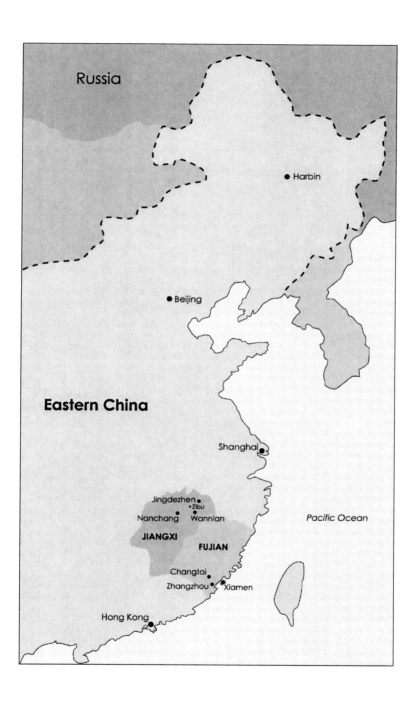

Prologue

When you are aware that you are the force that is Life, anything is possible. Miracles happen all the time, because those miracles are performed by the heart. The heart is in direct communication with the human soul, and when the heart speaks, even with the resistance of the head, something inside you changes; your heart opens another heart, and true love is possible.
Don Miguel Ruiz

No pessimist ever discovered the secret of the stars or sailed to an uncharted land or opened a new heaven to the human spirit.
Helen Keller

If not for the guidance of a still small voice, I would not have gone to China. If not for the inspiration of that voice, I would not have written this book. Both times the voice spoke in the first person and sounded like my own, though I was not the one formulating the words. Both times the message was delivered in a detached, matter-of-fact manner, its quality of knowing unquestionable.

The first time happened in January 2004, when my life in Canada was at an unbearable standstill. Loneliness, boredom and a sense of having no purpose were squeezing the life out of me, that is, until I heard an inner voice announcing that I was going to China. Within a few months I had taken a leave of absence from my job and found another in China. In the fall of 2004, my English teaching career in China began. I was planning to stay there for at least one school year. Then, in early 2005 after four months of teaching, I embarked on winter holiday travels with a bilingual friend.

Dancing in the Heart of the Dragon recounts my experiences on this holiday, which started with joy and ended with sorrow. In a poor rural area, the van I was travelling in met head on with a bus. After that accident, it took me well over a year to regain my normal walking ability.

Pinned in wreckage, I heard the still small voice again. It said: "I don't know what this is all about but I do know it's part of a bigger picture and it's a good picture and it involves me and China." Those simple words from a gentle, strong voice helped sustain me through much more trauma to come. Simple words from that wise and wonderful voice also helped lift me from despair and helped give me a purpose bigger than my life itself.

The good, the bad, the ugly and the wonderful. Indeed, I experienced them all. The accident, as intense and ugly as it was, plays a dramatic but small part in my story. The heart of China, as strong and vulnerable as it is, plays the bigger part. Now, from my own heart, I wish to share my story with you.

The Miracle of Getting Home

Jonathan scooped me up under the arms and Heather lifted me under the knees. I grabbed the bar beside the handicapped toilet and they lowered me. Jonathan left the airport washroom and Heather helped me a bit more before she left. They were mindful of providing me with at least some privacy, not that it mattered much to me anymore. After reversing the process and getting me back into the wheelchair, I marvelled at our accomplishment. Nine hours earlier, upon first arriving at Shanghai's Pudong Airport, it had taken three people twice as long to help me use the facilities. Relieved again and vowing to keep my fluid intake extremely low for the next eleven or so hours, I was ready to board the plane with Jonathan for our long flight back to Vancouver. With gratitude, I said goodbye to my Canadian friend Heather, who now lived in Shanghai. We'd only met once before, yet when I called her from Nanchang, she masterfully saw to a number of details, including the delicate call to be made to my family. I didn't want them to be more alarmed than necessary.

On the plane, a flight attendant helped Jonathan move me into a soft, wide seat. He had booked my ticket in the business class section, knowing I'd need the extra leg room. The airline upgraded his economy ticket so he could sit beside me. With legs extended over my luggage, cushions placed behind me and Dr. Zhao's last minute gift of a comforter tucked around me, I was surprisingly comfortable.

In awe, I looked at Jonathan. What an amazing human being he was. Only 26 years old, he'd taken charge of just about everything, including flying 2,200 kilometres from Harbin to Nanchang just a couple of days before in order to get me. Three officials from my university had accompanied him. Now he was seeing me safely back to Canada. Jonathan, a Mandarin-speaking Canadian, was a director for my employer's educational programs in China. From the first time we met, four months previously in Harbin, I had liked him. Now here we were, in the middle of an unexpected adventure half-way through our winter holiday.

Jonathan took out the packages of pills Dr. Zhao (not a medical doctor) had purchased for me in a Nanchang pharmacy. "Okay, Jonathan, how does it go? The yellow ones are sleeping pills; the blue ones are painkillers to be taken every four hours; and the white ones are antibiotics to be taken every six hours?" I didn't know the extent of my injuries. I did know my right side was the most traumatized. My leg was hugely swollen, knee inflamed and elbow bashed but not broken. The left side of my head had stitches and my bruised body ached all over. A Nanchang doctor had nonchalantly diagnosed a "minor fracture" of my right knee. With a specialist flown in from Beijing or Shanghai, they'd have me "up and walking in three weeks." That same doctor, who spoke English, also told me it was necessary to move from side to side in the hospital bed and try to sit up on my own. Really now?

My friend Yeming, who had also been in the accident, shared the hospital room with me. I was emphatic that if at all possible, I would stay in China. Yeming knew that and he wanted me to stay too. When he changed his mind and adamantly told me I needed to go back to Canada (because of something he'd overheard a doctor say), I knew something must be serious. The big question was how would I be able to return to Canada? In fact, three days after the accident I left China, flying from Nanchang to Shanghai, then from Shanghai to Vancouver. A different doctor came with us in an ambulance from the Nanchang hospital to the airport. When he examined my X-rays, his eyes widened and he pronounced that my going on an airplane was "*Not* a good idea."

The flight attendant brought our dinners. Jonathan unwrapped my cutlery and cut up the food on my plate. We talked for hours and I mellowed in the warmth of his loving care. I spoke about my two sons and daughter, and he told me about his family and other special people in his life in Eastern Canada. We talked about our beliefs, the *I Ching*, God. We also talked about wonderful and sometimes not so wonderful China, the "Land of the Dragon," with which we had both become enamoured. Reminiscing about the incredible Harbin International Ice and Snow Festival had us both smiling.

Jonathan and I on the flight from Shanghai to Vancouver

Then we talked about the "heavy-duty stuff" such as the details of the accident, about my travelling in the front seat of a van with no seatbelt and the bus smashing head on into us. "Everything was bizarre," I said to Jonathan. "The rescue with jaws-of-life crowbars, the surreal first hospital and that questionable second hospital you saw me in. And you know, when I was trapped in the wreckage, a voice told me everything would be better than okay. I need to believe that."

We talked about my friend Yeming, whose family slept on the floor for three nights to look after us, and about some unusual things that happened in that Nanchang hospital room. "Jonathan, leaving China is almost more than I can bear. Will I ever see my students and friends again? I know I need to return to Canada but it feels as though my heart's being ripped right out of my body."

Jonathan just looked at me. "Ramona, there's an expression in Chinese I want you to remember: *Da nan bu si, bi you hou fu*. It means that if you suffer a big bad event and it hasn't killed you, you will absolutely have great happiness in the future. It's better than luck, though it means you'll have that too." I hope so.

I cried when Jonathan said, "Ramona, you have no idea how many lives you touched in a meaningful way with your teaching, your openness, your willingness to embrace the new and your love." Before I fell asleep for a few hours with the aid of a sleeping pill, Jonathan said to me, "Look, if I'm asleep and you need something, you *must* wake me up. Promise?"

ooooo

Night yielded quickly to day and the late morning sun was shining when we arrived back in Canada at the Vancouver International Airport. An ambulance awaited me. When three paramedics came on board, I started to cry but had to stop. It hurt too much. "Finally I am safe, I am safe, I am safe. These people will really know what to do."

One paramedic, a big guy with long wavy brown hair and earrings, said, in a pseudo-gruff way, "Hey, my name's George. Those two guys over there are Warren and Glen," whereupon the two "guys" gave me a goofy look and announced:

"We're the Warren and Glen Show."

Oh, my God, now I was laughing but that hurt too much too. I was very happy.

"Where's the wheelchair?" I asked.

"We're not putting you in any wheelchair."

They lifted and placed me on a stretcher with a neck brace. *Kind of late for that*, I thought.

"Where are you taking me?"

"Richmond Hospital. It's the closest one. Is that okay with you?"

"Of course!"

Officials waved us through Customs, then I started talking all the way to the hospital. There was just so much for me to spill out. My lucidity was remarkable, I reflected.

Many people, family members and work associates, were waiting for me in Emergency. A young woman approached, crying profusely. I said to her,

"It's okay. Please don't cry." She continued crying. I asked, "What is your name?"

"Anna."

"That's interesting. I have a daughter named Anna, and she's about your age. How old are you?"

The sobbing turned to wailing, "Mom!"

Why is this young woman calling her mother over? I looked at her deeply tanned face and her braids. With a remorseful jolt, it hit me. So much for my lucidity. I had not recognized my own daughter.

Richmond Hospital, British Columbia

Pain ebbs and flows. Mostly it flows harder and harder, an out-of-control tide roaring towards a tiny shore. *Stop, right NOW! Where's that morphine?* The surging slows, the crash not so hard this time on my fragile frame. I have a chance to breathe a little. Ebb is too minuscule. *Brace yourself!* I press and press on that PCA thing, that "patient controlled analgesic" contraption. Nothing. The PCA is telling me, "Sorry. Too soon for more. You've got to wait." I don't want to crumble. Soon pain's constancy becomes my norm. Is it possible not to notice pain?

Monday, February 14, 2005, 9 p.m. Room 415

Catharsis

So much has happened and I vow to record it all, just not all at once. I arrived here yesterday afternoon. I keep telling people about what happened. It's like I can't keep it in. People just look at me with wide eyes.

Diagnosis—I'm a Little Broken

The Canadian doctors have confirmed seven broken ribs, two broken legs and a crushed right knee. When I met Dr. Arthur, he pointed at the right side of my chest and said, "That's what we're worried about." Then he pointed at my right knee and said, "Not that." I don't understand. Something about fluid pooled in my right lung.

Jonathan pretty much saved my life. He certainly succeeded in getting me out of China. The smug young doctor at that Nanchang hospital, supposedly the best hospital in all of Jiangxi Province, did not want to release me. (Too much face to save?) I "couldn't be moved," I had a "hip injury, blah, blah." The Chinese doctors ordered scads of X-rays at the end. Maybe that last set when the truth was revealed was the real reason they didn't want to let me go. I'd thought the pain in my chest and back came from muscles pulled badly as a result of clinging to that seat.

Morphine is grogging me out...

Tuesday, February 15, 2005, 8:35 p.m. Room 415, Richmond Hospital

Grumpy

Not feeling well. A couple of times today I crumbled with discouragement in the face of even more pain. Until now, I have been composed and accepting of slings and arrows with the kind of dignity and grace I like. I guess crumbling now is understandable considering it's been five (or is it almost six?)

full days since that nightmare accident. I am hopeless with time differences and the International Dateline. Still my mind is good, thank God. Dr. Arthur said there'd be no surgery tomorrow because of continued bad swelling. He told me that late yesterday afternoon as he was going home and I was being taken downstairs for a neck X-ray. I guess he forgot to correct that info in my file, so now I'm allowed nothing to drink or eat.

I have misplaced my glasses and can hardly see what I'm writing now. I'm lying on my left side (sort of) to take the pressure off my back. My right leg is wrapped securely in a tensor bandage. At times I feel I could SCREAM. My leg feels as though it's in the grip of a vice, there's so much swelling. I also stink. Acrid, sticky perspiration. My hair is a matted, filthy mess. I have big constipation bloat. Gee, I wonder if I am grumpy?

Wednesday, February 16, 2005, 2:40 a.m.

Awake

Can't get back to sleep so I've decided to turn the light on and write. My body thinks it's supper time tomorrow, China time. What good fortune that the first available bed was in a private room. It's spacious and comfortable, and there's a phone in here nobody has bothered to take away. A nurse said, "We're supposed to but we won't." Everybody is so nice, and it's not just the telephone thing.

I've had a fever for a day and a half. The window's open to clean, fresh B.C. air! Two laxatives last night were gross: cooked, mashed-up prunes, apples and white stuff—Maalox? It's succeeded in bloating me up even worse. Nausea's setting in. Oh for a hot tummy compress and a big drink of water.

"How Are You Still Alive?"

Dr. Arthur visited today. He told me he and his colleagues are trying to work out how to "put me back together." It's not exactly reassuring, though nurses tell me they're excellent surgeons.

Other leg fractures—right fibula and left tibial plateau—apparently have less displacement and will heal on their own. My peroneal nerve might be damaged as a result of the broken fibula. Dr. Arthur asked two questions I've been hearing a lot:

1. "How are you still alive?" I don't know. Why do people keep asking me that?

2. "What airline ever let you on board? Airlines don't let people in your condition on board." I don't know much about that either. I didn't mention that two airlines had.

PCA Fog and Clog and the Issue of Pain

I have a PCA, a "Patient Controlled Analgesic." It's morphine, the mixed blessing, with pain alleviation on the one hand, and fog and additional clogging of my system on the other. My tolerance for pain goes up and down. Much of the time, I'm pretty clear-headed. I have an IV for antibiotics and a catheter. Plus, there's a syringe of blood thinner for me to jab into my gut regularly. With all my bloating, I can barely feel it.

This business of pain and drugs puzzles me, especially in those last few days in China. My pain threshold is normally low, yet I didn't ask for medication except for the first night in Nanchang. It's strange. I felt a lot of pain but then maybe not as much as I might have, considering my injuries. Except for the injection from a nurse the first night and the pills from Dr. Zhao the last morning, I recall no other pain relief in China.

Maybe my body produced some trauma-shielding chemical that blocked out pain. I wonder if such a chemical exists. Or maybe I was in an altered state, dissociated, except I didn't have any experience of watching myself from outside my body. (Not then but I do now, when I remember.) I did experience crying and moaning and thinking the sounds came from somewhere else. Emotionally, not much seemed to faze me except when the people gawked at me when I was on the ground.

In a way I've found sanctuary in my mind. Not once did I think I was going to die. A couple of scary times I thought I might but not that I would. (Like when I was being carried up and then down three flights of stairs on a board. I can hardly bear to think of that.) Looking back now, it amazes me how together I was. I was present and seemed to roll with the punches. Or maybe I'm fooling myself, like when I didn't recognize Anna, my own daughter, here in Richmond. It's as though I was detached from my body rather than separated from it. Whatever was going on for me boils down to one word: survival.

Wednesday, February 16, 2005, 3:55 a.m.

Emulate the Way of Water

Lying here gives me plenty of time to think and also to sink into the depths of my emotions. Before Jonathan left a couple of days ago he told me to make sure I listen to a song called "The River" by Garth Brooks. He said I'd understand why when I heard it. Even though I haven't yet, his comment got me thinking. Like a river, my life was moving along. A good current was carrying me and I was swimming with it; that is, until a big explosion and a huge landslide. The river's blocked now and I'm going nowhere or so it seems. *Not a completely bad thing*, I must remind myself. Obstacles, according to one of the I Ching hexagrams, are an inherent part of one's life path and necessary for personal growth. The hexagram says that when cataclysmic things happen, it's good to emulate the way of water.

There's something about all this philosophy that has made perfect sense to me ever since I was introduced to the I Ching 15 years ago. I can feel the metaphors, not just think about them. It must be my poetic way of understanding things. Emulate the way of water? Water is soft. It's passive in as much as it needs gravity or wind or other natural phenomena to work upon it but it can't be said to be weak. The old question is: "Which is more powerful, rock or water?" The answer is water. Give it enough time and it will wear the rock away. Patience and steadfastness are the qualities I hear.

Similarly, the blockage of a river or stream is a time for pause, not idleness. It's a time for active inactivity. *Wei wu wei* I believe it's called. Oh I love the paradoxes of Chinese Taoist philosophy! Using time to build up its strength, a river will eventually have enough power to find a way around the landslide or flow over the top of it or even divert in a brand new direction, which may or may not mean a new destination. Whichever way it takes, a river flows in harmony with its course, its pathway. This must be what it means to follow one's Tao. So, if my life is indeed like a river, I need to peacefully build up my strength, with patience and a mind steadfast on recovery. A new direction may be mine with a destination that I can now only guess at. It's exciting if I think of it this way. Destination and destiny: I bet they are connected.

Nurse Jon

On another happy note, I realize I've not written about my favourite nurse. His name is Jon, he's Chinese, and he's sunshine itself! He walks in and starts fussing like an old mother hen. He's encouraging and he takes time to relate with me. A couple of days ago, he walked in with pseudo fanfare.

"Hooray, what a gas! We love gas around here. Didn't you know we're the gas factory?"

"Ha ha! Hey Jon, I like how there are so many Chinese people who work here."

"This is Richmond, remember? And thank you. It's nice to hear."

"You're welcome."

"What are you writing?"

"Journal entries. I don't know what I'd do without my journal."

"Me, I'm not a writer. I can see you like writing."

"Writing in my journal helps me remember things and make

sense of things too. Especially the bad stuff. Writing can help me turn my garbage into gold."

"Uh huh. Sounds pretty useful. I bet you've got some interesting things to say about China."

"I think so." I liked his interest.

"What took you there in the first place? Did you go there on a holiday?"

"No, I went to teach English for a year and I was on a holiday when the accident happened. I'd only been there four months, Jon. This is a rip-off. I didn't want to leave China."

"I'm sorry."

"Me too."

"Have you written anything about the accident yet?"

"Yeah, a fair bit. I wrote in the Nanchang hospital. It's good I didn't know about the accident in advance. I doubt I'd have had the guts to go to China."

"Have you written about how you got out of China?"

"A little. Everybody wants to know that. Everybody automatically assumes: 'So, they sent you back to Canada.' Nope. There's no *they*."

"You've got me curious."

"I would be too if I were you. I was on an amazing holiday before all this happened. I went from heaven to hell."

"That good, then that bad?"

"Jon, I've got enough to write a book."

"You do that, Ramona. It'll be your gold. When you've got it finished, tell me. I'll read it."

"You never know. I bet I have enough for two books."

"Then I'll read both."

"I appreciate your support, Jon."

Wednesday, February 16, 2005, 5:15 a.m.

Tapping into a Geyser

It's nearing dawn, a quiet time in which I've been reflecting on my day and my life. I've been thinking about my conversation with Jon and about my life as a river, as blocked as it may temporarily be. I am tired and peaceful yet, strangely, I notice a bubbly kind of excitement building up in me. I seem to be tapping into something deep: my desire to write and not just for myself. I want to write about me and China. Oh, in writing those last words down, I feel a geyser opening up! About me and China?

How will I ever be able to capture my feelings for China on paper? Explanations won't do it, plus they're boring. Only with the language of the heart might I succeed. How, though, does the heart speak? For me, through sensation—a prickling behind the eyes, an aching in the throat, a fluttering in the chest or a bubbling deep inside, opening up to a full-fledged geyser. Through sights and sounds, tastes and scents too. I shall write in prose, even though the spirit of poetry and song feels more appropriate.

This bed-ridden time is a gift. I have much to get down on paper: the past, even further-in-the-past and of course the present. I will need the ingenuity of a spider to weave my story. I must include what took me to China in the first place (*yes, Nurse Jon*) and at least something about my life in Harbin. My holiday, most definitely, and the accident, well that's what people will be extra curious about, I imagine.

What I have is time. What I need is strength.

Earlier

In early 2004, my life was not going well. My children had all left home, I'd ended a crazy-making relationship and the job I'd once found fulfilling had become tedious. I felt dried up and dead inside. That is, until I heard a voice. It was my own, in the first person, and it came as a thought. Calm and with a not-to-be-argued-with quality of authority, it simply stated, "I'm going to China." I said, "Yes." That was the easy part. The hows and the whats proved to be the hard part. For months I oscillated between trepidation and elation, enormously grateful for guidance from the *I Ching*, dreams, intuition, synchronicities: all forms of guidance from *the Presence*, what I also call *the All, Essence*, or *God*.

I took a leave of absence from my teaching job in Canada and accepted a teaching position on the other side of the Pacific. In early October 2004, I flew to Harbin, in Northeastern China. My life in this foreign land—the Land of the Dragon—with its ancient culture and unquenchable desire to catch up with the modern world, intrigued me. In my new regular job, Monday to Friday, I taught English to first-year students at the Harbin University of Science and Technology (HUST). In my Saturday afternoon job, I taught English conversation to master's students at the Study Abroad Center of the Harbin Institute of Technology (HIT). Through these jobs I met the young people who are central to my story. I met Yeming first, a master's student at HIT; next, Eria, a fourth-year English-major student at HUST. Through Eria I met Haiwu, also a HUST student soon to graduate with a degree in English. Eria and Haiwu were not my students, nor were they acquainted with Yeming who was my student. Just how we met comes later in my story.

From late January to the end of February, we had a five-week winter holiday and I wanted to see more of China. When Eria asked me to join her in travelling to Xiamen in Fujian Province, I said, "Yes!" My brief time in that southern coastal province turned out to be blissful. Then I travelled nineteen hours inland by train to meet Yeming near Jingdezhen in Jiangxi Province, one of China's poorest. His family had invited me to spend Spring Festival with them (often called Chinese or Lunar New Year) and I was very happy to accept. They lived in the countryside, across the river from a small town called Zibu. I quickly learned that *in the countryside* is a euphemism for "not very advanced." I stayed three days, up to and including Wednesday, February 9, Chinese New Year for 2005. On Thursday, February 10, on a dismal stretch of highway outside of Zibu, my exciting life in China came to an abrupt halt.

Preamble to Hell – Zibu, Jiangxi Province, PRC

Right after supper on Wednesday, February 9, I was told the family was having a New Year's party at their other home (a new place) across the river in Zibu proper. We got on the ferry, a raft-like vessel with a small sheltered area, powered by a motor that cut out a little too often for comfort, and crossed the river. Somehow the phenomenal amount of fun I had that night, dancing with about twenty-five young men, all family, fits perfectly. Late that night, I wrote in my journal: "I don't think I have danced so much in my entire life! Lots of karaoke and techno music. I literally let my hair f-l-y. Tomorrow I leave for the next 'leg' of my journey." (I really did put quotation marks around the word "leg." Weird.)

The following morning as I readied myself to depart, Yeming's father, Mr. Zhang, made a phone call to confirm the train ticket he'd managed to secure for me to Shanghai. I'd planned to stay there with my friend, Heather. Then Mr. Zhang wanted to know if I might not like to change my mind and stay longer. "Why?" I asked Yeming. The answer surprised me. "Because my father likes you." My stay had been all right but awkward. I was a foreigner staying with a traditional family who'd likely had few if any dealings with foreigners. As such, I had been excluded from several New Year's activities. *Maybe he likes me now because he got to see me as a real person last night*, was my thought. My limited views of my friend's father were soon to change. I told Yeming, "No, I really must go, but thank you."

With muddled feelings, I bid the family goodbye. Shanghai bound, I made my way to the ferry with Yeming and his cousin Haiming, and we crossed the river again to Zibu proper. We'd find a ride to the bigger town of Wannian, where they'd see me all the way to the train station. We made our way through muddy streets and approached a van driven by a man who provided a taxi service. The van was almost full already with about eight or nine people. The only passenger in the front got out, the driver and others insisting I take that seat. Despite the absence of a seat belt (one strap hung idly beside the seat), I reluctantly accepted. I tried to quell my uneasy feelings by recalling the 30-minute trip the opposite way, from Wannian to Zibu, only a few days before. I remembered the good quality paved road and the distinct lack of traffic. I also reminded myself, yet again, "This *is* China."

While travelling on roads in China, I'd developed the habit of narrowing or closing my eyes, holding my breath, and tensing my muscles—all part of the not-so-fine art of denial. In the big city of Harbin where I lived, I'd imagine myself in a movie with a few horn-honking crazies manoeuvring their way through traffic that included bicycles, three-wheeled taxis, cars, buses, trucks, motorcycles and horse-drawn wagons, as well as hundreds of pedestrians trying to cross roads. I imagined myself completely safe and all the danger around me simply unreal, just a movie I was watching. Such went my survival fantasy, my "movie." It's weird, ironic even, that I survived a head-on collision with none of these descriptors present. And it was a *fatal* collision, I found out a couple of days after the fact.

The driver was a jovial fellow, obviously pleased to provide transportation to a foreigner. He was curious about me. When I showed him a picture of my kids, he beamed all over and became very chatty in the local dialect. It didn't matter that I couldn't understand a word he said; I warmed up to him right away. Everybody else was friendly and talkative too. Yeming sat directly behind me, my heavy canvas travel bag between his knees and the back of my seat. Later he told me my bag, which ended up shredded, saved his legs. His cousin Haiming sat beside him. He later suffered a broken pelvis. The driver started the engine and we were off.

The day was chilly, drab and damp, maybe two degrees Celsius. We left Zibu at about 1:30 p.m. We drove through red-soiled, desolate-looking countryside. At one point, I saw a man at the side of the road urinating. I drew Yeming's attention to this. He told me, "Don't look. It's terrible." I think he was embarrassed.

Da Nan, the Big Bad Event

"Da nan bu si, bi you hou fu"—If you survive a disaster, then you will have good fortune and great happiness too.

About half an hour into our journey, I noticed chattiness being replaced by silence. I also noticed myself feeling sleepy, though I was awake. We were travelling at about 60-70 kph, by no means an excessive speed. In that half-hour I'd seen no other vehicle on the road. Then there was the bus, coming straight at us. I looked at our driver. His head was nodding. I realized we were on the wrong side of the road! I looked at the oncoming bus driver. He didn't pull over to the side of the road. Instead, he entered *his* wrong side to drive around us. Both vehicles were now on the wrong side. Our driver awoke and tried to correct his mistake. I shut my eyes.

C-R-A-S-H! Jarring, unreal. Whirlwind propulsion. A split second of blackness then electrifying sensation. I opened my eyes to find myself pinned between the passenger door and the crushed front of the van. My right leg was bent in a peculiar way. Some passengers screamed hysterically.

Our van driver's head was nodding but this time his mouth was dripping with blood and saliva. Turning my head, I looked upwards directly into the eyes of the driver of the bus that hit us. He was angled slightly to my right, looking down at us. After a minute or two, he backed his bus up. I did not see where he went but assumed he'd pulled over somewhere close by. I looked at my watch. It was almost 2 p.m. We waited.

Dozens of people materialized, seemingly out of nowhere. They stood beside the wreckage and stared at us, transfixed. People in the van continued to scream, yell and moan. After a while, it dawned on me that I was making sounds too. Over and over I pleaded, "Someone please help me." As far as I could tell, no one on the outside did anything.

I turned my head to see Yeming, noticed his lacerated face and said, "Oh, the driver, look at the poor driver." I wanted to touch him but he was slumped beyond my reach.

An old van showed up, which I figured was an ambulance. (In retrospect, I wonder if any emergency response existed at all. The van might have belonged to a private citizen. I'd like to know the men who freed me.) I could hear individuals being released from the back. At some point police came and walked around.

I waited and waited for what seemed like forever. My right leg especially was a raging inferno. Trapped and aflame with pain, I noticed what seemed a completely natural voice in my head, calm, matter-of-fact and detached from the horror. It said, "I don't know what this is all about but I do know it's part of a bigger picture and it's a good picture and it involves me and China."

Two men eventually came with crowbars. When they managed to pry the passenger door off, I almost fell out of the wreck backwards with my leg still trapped. Somehow I lurched forward and upwards, grabbed the back of the passenger seat, and clung for dear life. The impassive crowd continued to gawk. I begged Yeming, who'd obviously stayed with me, "Please, tell someone to help me. I need someone to support my weight." He tried but his attempt was feeble and futile. I clung with all my strength and waited. Ten minutes? Half an hour? An hour?

Finally two more men came and freed my leg. They picked me up and I went insane, hyperventilating and screaming. Much more and I'd have passed out. (I have replayed this scene many times since, as though I'm watching myself on a movie screen. The sight and my screams just about undo me every time. Each time I need to tell myself, *better not watch that movie*.)

The men carried me down the road, sat me on a stack of concrete bricks and leaned me up against a building. Once again, standing a few feet away, people watched me. I closed my eyes to block them out. How long did I wait? Two different men arrived and pointed at me as if to say, "Hey, here's this one." They picked me up and honestly tried to be careful but I started hyperventilating again. They carried me to the other side of the road, gently laid me on the muddy ground and shoved some straw under my head. By now it was drizzling. The onlookers hovered about with their open umbrellas. Not one so much as tried to shield me from the rain. I could barely take their unabashed nosiness and their seeming indifference. I closed my eyes to block them out. Mortified, I could have died then and there.

At long last the old van returned for me, the last casualty. Two men picked me up and plopped me upright onto a passenger seat in the middle. Thus I was transported to the little hospital in the town of Wannian.

Don't tell me that's a stretcher? I thought, as I saw the board, about 18 inches wide. It must have been thick because it held my weight. Two men placed me on it and carried me into the freezing-cold, dilapidated building. No gurney awaited us, neither did an elevator. I gripped the sides of the board, held my breath, and prayed as the two little men carried me up two or maybe three flights of stairs.

A surreal experience awaited me. The men brought me into a room teeming with people and I was eased off the board onto a bed. Yeming was there, as were his father, mother, 29-year-old sister, Yanhong, and numerous adult male cousins I'd danced with the night before. In addition there were others I didn't know. My being a foreigner aroused a lot of interest. Yeming's mother wept and pointed at her son. He explained, "My mother says she feels very sorry for what has happened to you. She says my condition is worse than yours."

Really? I knew I must be in bad shape; if Yeming was in worse shape, then I felt awful. *But he's standing and walking,* I considered. (I never did figure out exactly what his injuries were other than the facial cuts. I knew he could walk but had trouble lying down and could not get up on his own. A broken collar bone or ribs? He never wanted to talk about it.)

About this time an attractive young woman walked into the room. She spoke English and told me I could call her Sophie. She was a local school teacher who taught English and had been asked to help me. What would I ever have done without translation assistance?

A police officer arrived. I told Yeming, "Please tell the officer I saw everything. I can tell him everything that happened."

Yeming translated the officer's response, "Forget it. It doesn't matter."

No sooner had the policeman walked away than someone presented me with a gigantic, gorgeous bouquet of fresh cut roses and other flowers.

"What's this?" Then another person presented me with an enormous basket of fresh fruit.

"What is this?"

"These are for you," Sophie said.

"Who would be giving me flowers and fruit?"

"These are from the province of Jiangxi to say how sorry they are you got hurt."

"Oh."

That was it. Flowers and fruit were placed on a table behind me. Never again did I see either. Likely just forgotten, like my shoes. Somebody took my footwear off. Yeming explained how my pants had to be cut off. Strange that with all the things for me to worry about, I should choose to fixate on my especially loved black denims. They happened to be the only pants I had while travelling, not that it mattered anymore.

"Please, Yeming, tell them to cut only along the seams. That way I can get them fixed later." No such luck, of course. My lower clothes were destroyed—jeans and long underwear made of expensive merino wool.

My top clothes, luckily, covered half my thighs. I lay on top of the remnants, shivering, and refrained from looking at my smashed right leg. Someone rolled an ancient X-ray machine into the room and the people gathered round. Either lack of knowledge or flagrant disregard for the hazards of radiation prevailed.

I just lay there. With no heat in the building and my legs bare for the world to see, it was no wonder I almost froze. I looked up at a high dirty window, the one where the glass didn't seem quite flush with its frame. The way cleared and a man brought a strange long white piece of hard plastic to my bed. It was a splint of sorts. The back extended almost as high as my knee or just past my knee. The foot part curved to the right, indicating it was meant for a left leg and foot. My right leg was secured to this item. (Later when I arrived back in Canada, doctors and nurses all asked me the same question: "What is that thing?") The Wannian hospital was small, and they were doing their very best for me.

The doctor, now holding X-rays, spoke to Yeming, who translated for me.

"The doctor says you have a broken knee."

"Oh."

"He wants to send you to a better hospital in the capital city."

"Oh."

"You are allowed to make demands."

"Oh. What do you mean?"

"Anything you demand, you can have."

"Pardon?"

26

Yeming repeated his last statement.

"I don't get it. What do you mean?"

Yeming pretty much repeated himself yet again.

"Please give me an example."

"Well, you could demand to go to a better hospital and demand for me and my family to come with you." I realized a more accurate translation for "demand" would have been "request."

"Yes, this is what I want. And if it's a better hospital, then of course I want that for you too." The matter was decided.

The doctor was kind and vastly more human than the next two I was to encounter in the *better* hospital. He wanted to know who he should contact on my behalf. I handed him my cell phone and pointed to the number of Xing Baoshan (Steve), a man at my university in Harbin. The doctor immediately phoned.

Next came the reverse trip down the flights of stairs on the stretcher. I don't even want to think about that. I was laid on the floor of a van. I can't remember if the wooden stretcher was still under me or not. Neither have I any recollection of a blanket or someone's coat covering my legs but there must have been something. Yeming's relatives: his father, his sister Yanhong, and his 27-year-old male cousin Jingming, along with Sophie, the local school teacher, seated themselves around me. Then Yeming's mother and his other male relatives who'd been in the hospital room leaned down to take my hand and say good-bye. I felt very emotional. One of Yeming's cousins was beside himself with distress and didn't want to let go. We looked at each other imploringly, not wanting any of this awfulness to be true.

I was told the trip to Nanchang would take an hour. I looked at my watch. It was almost 8 p.m. or was it 9? The trip was quiet and monotonous in a soothing sort of way. The driver tried to negotiate the bumps in the road as gently as possible for which I thanked him, "*Xie xie ni.*" I knew a few words and phrases in Mandarin. Soon we were on smooth pavement. We arrived at the Nanchang University Medical Hospital #2 shortly before 11 p.m.

or was it 10 p.m.? Whichever it was, I noted the trip had taken two hours.

The 'Better' Hospital

Heaven itself—there was heat! The hospital was definitely several notches up. It was luxury compared with the first hospital but it was still dirty. I was lifted onto a gurney and an elevator took us up to the fourth floor. People were lying on the hallway floor. They were not patients but caregivers, I found out later. We entered a room with two beds. There was no transfer board here either. I was put onto the bed nearer the window. The other bed was for Yeming.

No such thing as towels or cloths or soap were available in the room's little washroom but there was hot water. Yanhong went through my belongings and found a face cloth. In the washroom she found a little metal bowl, filled it with hot water, and with my cloth started to wash my face and hands. Gasping, she called to Yeming, who told me blood was pooled in my left ear. Yanhong then discovered a gash about 3 or 4 inches above that ear and ran to find a doctor.

The doctor, maybe in his 50s, was none-too-nice and came across as angry, as a matter of fact. He examined my head, grabbed and yanked on a handful of my hair, then cut it off forcefully with what seemed a dull knife or dull pair of scissors. He then proceeded to stitch the wound roughly. Either I heard or imagined I heard, a crunching sound with each poke of the needle. I gritted my teeth. When the doctor was done, he jabbed at the area with a cotton ball of disinfectant, then threw the ball on the floor and stomped out. What was I to make of this flagrant ill-temper? It was Chinese New Year. Maybe few doctors were on duty and this one was angry due to overwork. Was he resentful because he'd rather be home with his family? Was he paid abysmally? If I wanted decent care, should I have handed him a wad of money at the outset? Somebody once told me that.

I was a foreigner so maybe I was rich but I had given him no money.

A nurse came in with an IV and a tray with other paraphernalia. I worried about the cleanliness of the needles and looked to Yeming and Sophie for an answer. "Safe?" I asked. What could they say? I decided I had to trust they were okay. The nurse took blood samples from my left arm and on the back of my left hand inserted an IV needle. Antibiotics, I was informed. The nurse also gave me a tetanus shot, then left.

Soon another doctor entered the room. I was, unfortunately, very concerned about the state of my gut. I'd been on a 19-hour train ride four or five days before, followed by three days in a home with no toilet, only a plastic pail. It had all ensured a complete shutdown of that detox system in my body. Now I was flat on my back and for how long?

Reluctantly and boldly I asked, "Can I have an enema"?

This doctor, though he could speak some English, answered in Chinese. Sophie translated.

"Ramona, he says you will get an infection."

"Oh! In that case, I want a laxative."

A tablet was brought to me, which helped a bit the next morning.

This doctor was much younger and smiled in a way that I wasn't comfortable with; neither was I comfortable with his smug manner. He'd been in the USA, where he'd learned some English. He said my injury was not serious.

"You have minor break of right knee. So many my patients have same." Here he gestured his arm vaguely toward the door. "We get doctor from Beijing o' Shanghai. You be up walking in three weeks. You must move side to side. You don't want sores." The fact of the matter was I could not move my upper body on my own.

My cell phone rang. It was my colleague and friend in Harbin, Jonathan. "Ramona, three others from HUST and I are coming to get you out. We'll be arriving tomorrow night." Xing Baoshan must have informed him.

Get me out? I didn't understand but the fact he and others from my university were coming, and from so far away, felt reassuring.

I had not received any relief for pain up until this point. It was maybe midnight, so about 10 hours since the accident.

"I want morphine," I said to the smug young doctor.

"We don't have morphine."

"What do you mean you don't have morphine? In Canada I can have morphine."

He shrugged and left. A few minutes later, a different nurse showed up and injected something into my left buttock, an analgesic I suppose, since some of the pain diminished.

Since morning I'd not had anything to eat or drink, nor had I emptied my bladder since noon. I wanted no food but welcomed a little water. Yanhong, assuming the role of a caregiving nurse, uncomplainingly helped me. She found a bedpan. Reaching under the covers, she pulled down my underwear. Her father and Jingming, looking the other way, discreetly lifted my butt for her to slide the bedpan under.

I'd only been slightly acquainted with these people for three days and here they were, two men and one woman, taking care of my very personal needs. As regards my having any modesty, the answer is yes and no. Practically speaking there was no need for it since this was survival. Emotionally speaking, I felt very humble and also very appreciative. They knew and wanted to help me as best they could.

I'd had no idea that requesting Yeming and his relatives to come with me to Nanchang would prove so critical. They obviously knew it would be. I came to realize a hospital nurse's role was to bring medication, give injections and take blood. Their role did not include providing personal care. This is why the hospital's floors served as sleeping areas for the friends and families of patients. Without them, there would be virtually no assistance, food, drink, washing or bedpan. When talking about hospitals, a friend in Harbin had once told me, "If you don't have family or friends, you might as well stay home and die."

It was well past midnight. Yeming got help to lie down on the other bed. Yanhong slept on top of her brother's bed the opposite way, with her head at its base. She used her coat as a blanket. Mr. Zhang and Jingming settled on the hard floor. Sophie stayed that first night too. It's hard for me to imagine her sleeping on the floor but there was nowhere else. I doubt they had blankets or pillows.

Someone turned the light off. I lay hovering in a state somewhere between sleep and wakefulness. Throughout the night I could hear loud moaning that seemed to come from the hallway or another room, that is, until reality sank in. I was the one moaning.

Daylight in Nanchang

The first morning, Friday, I looked up through the high streaky window of the hospital room to see the winter grey sky of Nanchang, about all I ever saw of that city. Busyness was to fill this day, as well as a suspended kind of exhaustion. I remember events but their sequencing is now fuzzy. No matter. Understandably, Sophie left. She needed to go home to her little girl. With Yeming's fluency in English, there was no reason for her to stay. I was sorry to hear she had no e-mail address and unfortunately I didn't get her Chinese name or phone number. If I can ever bring myself to return to Wannian, I shall look for her.

Yanhong showed me my small backpack, which I had filled tight with personal belongings before I left. It contained a water bottle, and a few pounds of fruit—oranges, bananas, apples, plus fruits distinctly Chinese that friends had insisted I take. What a mess! Almost everything was covered in "pureed" fruit. The water bottle was crushed, my pens were broken and so were my glasses. Luckily I could still use them. My soft covered journal was crunched but otherwise intact and undamaged by moisture, thank goodness. Yanhong cleaned up the mess, turned the pack inside out, washed it and hung it near the radiator. Jingming showed me my heavy canvas travel bag, the one Yeming had secured between his legs and the van's front passenger seat. I was astonished to see it had been demolished.

My right leg, ankle and foot continued to swell noticeably. I experienced almost intolerable pressure and pain mingled with numbness. If only I could experience some sensation. I desperately wanted someone to touch my leg and especially my dead-weight, freezing-cold, traumatized foot. No one cared to. Yeming answered no when I despairingly asked, "Is there a superstition in China about touching someone else's foot?"

I figured all my other pain and weakness resulted from severe bruising and pulled muscles. I could only move my arms and head. When I felt up to it, others lifted me to sit, putting pillows behind my back. When I tired, they laid me back down. In either position, sitting or lying, I was thankful to have my cell phone.

Since I had only a minor fracture, I didn't want to leave China. Still, because it was the required thing to do, I tried calling my Canadian travel insurance provider. The call could not be processed, no matter how many times I tried. I handed the phone and the wallet card they'd given me to Yeming. He wasn't successful either. Each time the recorded message in Chinese followed by English said, "Please try your call again later." I told myself not to worry.

I turned my attention to my friends in China. First I phoned Eria, who was back in Harbin. She was practical and quickly saw to the addition of lots of air time on my cell phone. Next I called Haiwu, still at his parents' home in Chang Tai, near Xiamen, where I'd stayed for about ten days. He hadn't planned on returning to Harbin for at least another two weeks but said, "I'll get a train back to Harbin and detour to Nanchang so I can see you as soon as possible."

I called Dan, my Israeli professor friend at Heilongjiang

University in Harbin, and asked him if he'd tend to certain matters for me. His offer of money to help if I needed any touched me. Then I called my friends Liyi and Songhe in Harbin. Tim, an American I'd met in Chang Tai, was next. He had the presence of mind to link me up with the Canadian Embassy in Beijing. A Miss Tian started a file on me and the accident. They'd know who I was in case I needed their help.

Throughout the day, one person would stay with me while the others went out. Yeming was able to come and go. Very weary, I rested between phone calls and journal writing.

Anxious for me to eat, Yeming and his family asked me several times what I'd like. "Nothing." The thought of food made me ill. "I only want water or unsweetened orange juice." Even then I didn't want to drink much because that meant the bedpan. With much coaxing, I agreed to some noodle soup. Over the course of that day and the next, they brought me soup a few times. Each time I took a little broth and pushed the rest away.

Yanhong had prepared another basin of warm water and my face cloth, when the smug young doctor came into the room again. He pointed to the IV puncture mark and said, "Don't get wet." *What's the big deal?* I wondered. Then I understood. *Tap water, of course. I could get an infection.*

In the early evening, Jonathan called again. "Ramona, we're at the Beijing Airport, waiting for a connecting flight. I'll call you when we arrive." It seemed like no time at all when he next called to tell me he and the HUST administrators had arrived but it was late, 10 p.m. They were staying in a hotel beside the hospital and would see me in the morning.

The next day, Saturday, my last full day in China, was a whirl of craziness.

Saturday, February 12, 2005, 3:40 p.m. University Medical College Hospital #2 Nanchang

All Real and So Unreal

Tomorrow I start my trip back to Canada. I have not been able to reach the travel insurance company. Business class at the last minute from Shanghai to Vancouver is costing me almost $3,000. I gave Jonathan my credit card number. HUST is paying for the first flight from Nanchang to Shanghai. I think I'm in shock. The magnitude of the accident hasn't sunk in. Today I found out our driver died. I'd watched him die and hadn't realized it. I also found out the bus driver drove away. "No, he didn't," I said. Inconceivable. All real and so unreal.

The day started early when Jonathan, Dr. Zhao (the director of HUST's International College), Mr. Sun (assistant director), and Miss Zhang crammed into the room. Yeming's father and Jingming were still asleep on the floor. The HUST people looked aghast. Jonathan explained if the accident had happened in Harbin, their "considerable" influence could have got me better care. Because Harbin's 2,000+ km away, their influence amounts to nothing here. Tomorrow I start my trip back to Canada. (Oh yeah, I already wrote that.) I am confused. Doctors here told me my injury's not serious. I don't want my family to freak out. I phoned Heather in Shanghai, told her what had happened and asked her to call Rachelle and hope her husband answers the phone. I told her to make it clear I am okay.

Dr. Zhao's a "take no bullshit" kind of woman. She gave Yeming hell, big time. She hadn't met him before. They're not even at the same university. It was horrible. Jonathan translated: "Why didn't you look after her? It was your duty to make sure nothing bad happened to her!"

I asked Jonathan to tell her it wasn't Yeming's fault. She just yelled more. Yeming looked demolished. I told him, "It was not your fault. I'm your friend. What matters most is you never ever blame yourself."

Haiwu arrived when everybody was still crowded in the

room. He had less than two hours before he needed to return to the train station. I introduced him as my friend from Chang Tai. Poor Mr. Zhang. I don't think he knew what to think. The look on his face seemed to say: *Who is this Ramona person anyway? First 'important' people fly from Harbin to help her. Then a young man about the same age as my son comes a long way to see her.* Haiwu was eager to help me and said he'd buy anything I wanted. I told him only orange juice, but unsweetened. He couldn't find any so bought me sweetened orange juice and several bottles of water.

X-Ray Insanity

Haiwu was here during the awfulness of the X-ray time and so was Jonathan. What a horrible charade. A couple of men came with a gurney, picked me up, and I went insane. Unskilled people in this place will kill me? Haiwu and Jonathan came with me down to the X-ray department. A nurse held my IV and many people came in to watch. Nobody was protected. Jonathan and Haiwu stood outside the room. Jonathan told me the conversation he had afterwards with, I think, a doctor.

"Why weren't those people told to leave?"

"What difference does it make?"

"And what about that nurse?"

"She holds the IV for everyone getting X-rays. That's her job." Unreal.

Truth About a Lie

Those were the first X-rays taken at this hospital. Yeming told me something shocking after. The truth about a lie? He said, "I overheard the doctor. He lied to you. Your condition is serious. It's good you are going home to Canada. You need to go." What is the truth?

I have no pants and forgot my shoes with expensive orthotics at the last hospital. Jonathan went out and bought me tear-aways meant for a big person, good considering the size of my leg and the splint thing. Dr. Zhao bought me a comforter, pale blue. Maybe it will prove helpful to move me.

35

She also bought lots of medication.

I hated to see Haiwu leave. I said, "Remember when I left Chang Tai? You told me the next place would be even better and I said, 'If it's half as wonderful, I'll consider myself blessed.' Look at me now, Haiwu! I will come back to China. I promise." I could cry for the amazing friend he is. Bless his beautiful heart.

After Haiwu left, Jonathan was the only person in the room with me. He surprised me by asking if I'd like him to brush my hair! "I've never done it before. My girlfriend will be happy if I learn." Another beautiful young man. He started brushing on the right side, gently. Some Chinese women stood in the doorway to watch. I hardly seemed to notice them anymore and usually try to ignore them when I do.

Jonathan said, "I'm going to tell them to get lost."

I said, "No, it's okay," and waved them over.

I had one massage my left leg and the other comb my matted hair on the left side. Astounded? I could imagine them later saying, *And that foreigner! She even invited us in and asked us to touch her!* I told Jonathan, "If they want to gawk, I might as well put them to work."

They had a million questions and Jonathan finally told them to leave. "Ramona, they were too nosey. They wanted to know where Yeming and his family were from and how much money they had. Gossip machines. They asked if you and Yeming were lovers." *Oh God, is this absurd or what?*

Jonathan said, "I can't believe you, Ramona. Any other foreigner in your situation, in so much pain and in such a filthy, disgusting place would be screaming and swearing their head off. I haven't heard you complain even once. You're just nice to people."

I don't understand that myself either. I'm in an altered state, most likely.

Saturday, February 12, 2005 8:50 p.m.

Who is This Man Really?

How can I write? I'm exhausted. This place is noisy with radiator rumbling and hallway racket. After Jonathan finished brushing my hair and left around 2 or 3 p.m., Mr. Zhang took a turn staying in the room with me. I wonder what we'd say to each other if we could. I sense there's been much misunderstanding. Compared to a few days ago, we are seeing each other with radically different eyes. It's like a meeting of unspoken ways. He knows almost nothing about me and I almost nothing about him. From poverty and Old-World mentality to New World affluence, yes I get that. But who is this man really?

After a few minutes, Mr. Zhang gestured that he'd like to help sit me up. He had some soup, which I didn't want. His eagerness for me to eat something was apparent and I didn't want to hurt his feelings, so I nodded. Gently but firmly he placed his hand under my back and sat me up. I tried to ignore the people watching from the doorway yet again. Mr. Zhang brought me the soup, some noodles and broth in a disposable container. After I drank a little broth, he helped me lie back down.

Robbed

I couldn't believe what happened next. It was like a scene from a Kafka novel, with Mr. Zhang suddenly going berserk! He ran out into the hallway screaming. Other voices thundered, then two policemen strode into the room. Different people were hauled in, men and women. Jonathan and Yeming returned.

"Police want to know who else was in the room, Ramona. Who do you recognize?"

"Yeming, some don't look familiar at all. Some do. Like that man there. For all I know, he was in here a different time. I don't know. Tell me what happened."

"My father was robbed. When he was helping you, somebody took his briefcase from the other bed. Lots of money was in it."

"How much?"

"20,000 rmb." Well over $3,000.

"How come so much?"

"My father's a businessman and was going to do business in this city."

Last Night and Day in China

I could not continue to write anything more in the Nanchang hospital due to exhaustion. I shall pick up where I left off—a robbery and police in my hospital room. It was a scene from an Abbott and Costello movie, except that it wasn't funny. It wasn't even incongruous, considering how weird the situation already was.

I felt very sorry for Mr. Zhang, blind-sided while he was busy being kind. He looked dazed. That evening he was so upset he refused to eat. Jonathan told me what Yanhong said.

"Father, money comes and goes but if your health goes, you might never get it back. You need to eat. Your family is what is important and you need to set a good example for us." Mr. Zhang sighed, put his head down and then ate something.

Since I'd be leaving early in the morning at about 5:30, a nurse delivered my bill that night. I insisted on paying for it but Mr. Zhang was equally as insistent that he pay. Pride and saving face are important, so I asked Yeming to try to explain that my Canadian medical services plan would reimburse me. Even if it wouldn't, I'd never tell them. Finally Yeming got him to agree to my paying half. I kept the invoice, all in Chinese. I'll be interested later, after I get it translated, to find out what they charged me for.

Wo Ai Ni Men

That night, the Zhangs all sat on the other bed, Dad with his son and daughter and his nephew Jingming. Nobody said anything for a while. Tenderness filled the air. Emotion filled me as I looked at these humble, dear people who'd given me their all. Would I ever see them again? I decided to tell them something I'd learned from a song, and I meant it. "*Wo ai ni men.*" ("I love you guys.")

Oh my, that blew them right out of the water. They looked everywhere but at me, that is, until their embarrassment subsided. I looked at Mr. Zhang, pointed at Yeming, and did two thumbs up.

"*Haojile!*" ("Wonderful—You have a wonderful son.") Mr. Zhang's eyes widened with astonishment. Yeming looked me straight in the face.

With all his heart in his voice, he said, "Thank you, Ramona."

Then shy, solemn and completely unpretentious, they all looked at me. I shall never forget.

The "How" of Leaving

Getting out of China was difficult. I still don't know how Jonathan, Dr. Zhao and the others got the hospital to release me. We started to get ready at 5 a.m. I had so much pee in me I thought, *Heck, I don't care if I overflow the bedpan*, and I did. Yanhong put an adult diaper on me. There was no way, if I could help it, I'd need it.

Jonathan arrived. Dr. Zhao and the others would take a taxi and meet us at the Nanchang Airport. Jonathan braced his arms around me from behind, under my arms, and someone else lifted me under both knees. I was put on a loosely woven stretcher on a gurney. Thank goodness for Dr. Zhao's comforter. It provided a slight buffer between my body and the stretcher placed on the ambulance floor. I said goodbye to my Chinese friends. *Will I ever see them again?* I reached out and took Yanhong's hands and said,

"Thank you, sweetheart." She didn't need to know English to understand me.

A different doctor came in the ambulance with Jonathan and me. After the smug young doctor, I was wary about believing another doctor. This one looked shocked when he showed us the X-rays—broken ribs. First I'd heard of it. I should stay in China, he said. Jonathan and I understood there was a risk but just what it was, we didn't know. All we knew was that it was imperative to get me out.

The ambulance attendants placed me flat on the floor in the middle of the Nanchang airport. The airline had agreed to let me fly and then changed their mind. "No way, she can't sit." Thank God for Jonathan. He sat me up. They relented. *Phew!*

I was put in an airport wheelchair and taken up a ramp onto the plane. Jonathan and I had bulkhead seats. With legs extended and propped up on my luggage, which was conveniently held together with a rope, I was able to be comfortable. Dr. Zhao was amazing with all the pills she'd bought for me the night before. She and the two others sat behind Jonathan and me.

Arrival at Shanghai's Pudong Airport was a delicious taste of civilization. I was seated in another wheelchair. Jonathan and I were lowered onto the tarmac by a special elevator. The three from HUST met us and the two women and Jonathan helped me in a wheelchair-accessible washroom.

We spent several hours at a refreshment bar just talking. While Miss Zhang braided my hair, Mr. Sun joked that if I needed someone in the airport to help me, all I needed to do was tell them I was Dr. Norman Bethune's niece. I liked Mr. Sun. He made me smile, especially when he laughed at his own jokes. Jonathan prompted me to sing the chorus, the only three lines I know of "*Lao Shu Ai Da Mi*" ("Mice Love Rice.") Mr. Sun quickly found the song on some mobile device and handed it to me. I sat listening over and over, head down, tears rolling down my face. It was the first time my leaving really hit me.

Before the three people from HUST left to return to Harbin, the vice-president of the university called to extend best wishes to me for my recovery. I felt utterly bowled over by his kindness. The kindness of the other people from my university touched me deeply too.

Heather showed up. What a dear person for her practicality and thoughtfulness. She knew I'd lost my shoes in the Wannian Hospital and had found me some soft suede, crepe-soled footwear—needed only for my left foot, mind you, but still most helpful. Twenty yuan, about $3!

"I managed to reach your sister's in North Vancouver. Don't worry. Her husband answered. I downplayed everything like you asked." They'd been informed. That was the main thing.

I used the toilet one last time and managed all the way to Vancouver, about eleven hours away.

Recovery

Wednesday, February 16, 2005, 7:50 p.m., Richmond Hospital, British Columbia

Bits and Pieces

My heart is battered and aching, maybe more than my body. I am profoundly sad. My amazing life in China has come to this. I read and I remember, and I cry. Crying is good. Sometimes I feel what I'm going through is too difficult, a test of endurance. Tomorrow Dr. Arthur will operate on my knee, eight days after the accident.

Saturday, February 19, 2005, 1:45 p.m.

Flashback Back into Horror

A horrendous crashing sound jars the silence and my blood turns to ice water in my veins. A van and a bus are smashed face to face. Jagged metal and broken glass lie strewn on the road.

Oh my God! Passengers are helped out then I see the woman trapped. The men with crowbars come to pry the door off but still she's stuck. I can't bear to watch but cannot turn away either. They carry her out. Her screaming unnerves me. Nothing so unearthly have I ever...what!?

Oh! I'm not there. I'm here. Pain rages through my extremities and in my insides too. What?

Oh, the phone is ringing. Where is it?

"Hello."

"Mom! Mom, what happened?!"

"Daniel?"

"Mom, I just heard you were in an accident. Are you okay? Mom!"

Dan has just returned from California. He was on a University of Victoria reading break. I told him about the surgery Thursday afternoon. He said he'd aim for the 5:00 ferry, so I'll see him tonight. Nothing could please me more right now.

Beautiful Gifts

Before I go back to sleep, I want to mention that my aunt, Heather and her husband, Carl visited. Heather's a nurse at the Royal Columbian Hospital and without my even saying anything, she undid the bandaging around my right foot, applied lotion and massaged. I thought I'd gone to heaven. Her action reminded me of the last person who took such initiative, Haiwu's mom with my wrist. Two natural born healers. In addition to that beautiful gift, Heather and Carl brought me a discman, so now I can listen to the CDs I bought in China plus all the ones they've lent me.

Another gift I received was from three lovely ladies, who washed my hair as I lay in bed. The last time I washed it was ten days ago. It took four lathers to remove all the China mud, etc. One sang, "Got to wash that China right out of my hair." I don't think so. They removed the stitches from above my left ear and combed my hair out.

Surgery

It had been two days since the surgery on my right leg and knee. Dr. Arthur stopped by to provide me with details. Not everything has sunk in. When he mentioned a cadaver, I seemed to stop listening.

"It went much more smoothly than we anticipated. Sorry, but we had to cut through your quad muscle too."

"It'll heal?"

"Over time. Not looking at anything fast here. We put over a thousand dollars' worth of hardware in your leg—titanium steel."

"Will it come out later?"

"No. Watch out for the metal detectors in airports. You'll have quite the scar."

"Souvenir to tell me I didn't imagine everything."

"Didn't need to use any bone from you. We used artificial bone graft instead."

"What's that made from?"

"...partly harvested from a cadaver." Dr. Arthur gave me a fuller answer but this is the only part I recall.

Stuff

My leg was gigantically swollen, well bandaged and not in a cast. I hurt more than I had previously and wondered if that were possible. My body was severely compromised and what was I doing? Fretting over the small stuff. I was concerned about all my belongings in China, from both my office and apartment in Harbin. I was informed my things would be packed up for "safe-keeping." I considered strangers handling my things and "my" apartment's not being "mine" any longer. I hadn't said goodbye. I sent word to Charles to please look after my journals, *I Ching* books, photos, CDs and DVDs. I was also concerned about everything on the hard drives of both office and apartment computers; other stuff didn't matter as much as these things.

All these thoughts made me feel very sad. I needed to lift myself out of despair so went inward.

"God, this matter is beyond my control and isn't that important, I know that. Please help me shift out of energy-depleting thoughts."

"Relax, Ramona. Think of the river, flow with it. All is well. Relax."

"Right. Relaxation will help me to heal. I'll breathe you in and the worry out. Thank you, God."

Yes, time for me to b-r-e-a-t-h-e.

Bloating

Not only was my leg huge but also my poor tummy. My sister Rebecca visited and commiserated with me. I lamented,

"I feel old, tired, enormous and miserable. Bloat is getting to be a massive understatement. Be honest—how many months pregnant do I look?"

"I wasn't going to comment. Six, maybe seven. Must be awfully painful."

"The worst pain in my body. My last 10 days in China didn't help."

"The different kinds of food?"

"I don't know, maybe. I mean the toilets. One place had a squat toilet I didn't know how to flush and the other place had no toilet at all. Only a pail to share."

"You've got to be kidding!"

"I tend to shut down with travelling anyway."

"No wonder you've got a problem. It can't be the cause of this, though. There's got to be something else going on."

"Maybe the drugs. I hear morphine's deadly for binding the system. I need to stop taking it but the rest of me hurts too much. People talk about the essentials as being food, water, shelter. What about elimination? That's detox."

"Right."

"If I had to, I'd take squat toilets any day to have a mobile body that works well in that department."

"Have you seen a specialist yet?"

"No, but I requested one."

Specialist

A gastroenterologist did visit me later, a Dr. McFarlan. He was very nice.

"Ms…"

"No, please, call me Ramona."

"In that case, you must call me Mac."

I doubted I'd feel comfortable enough to do that, but his comment helped me feel more at ease. We chatted briefly, not that there was much he could say at that point.

Daniel

My son arrived after supper that night with an overnight bag and his guitar. We hadn't seen each other in six months. He sat beside the bed and held my hand. I told him about a weird, unsettling realization.

About Mom and Me

"Dan, almost nine years ago my mom died. Twelve years before that, she got a brain disease."

"Yeah, what was it called again?"

"*Herpes simplex encephalitis.* She was severely brain damaged for the rest of her life. Do you know how old I am? The same age as she was when she got the disease. I used to wonder what would happen to me when I was 53. When I decided to go to China, I figured, 'Nothing, because I'm creating an amazing life for myself!'"

"Mom?"

"I did some calculating with dates. Get this. Mom was 53 years, 5 months and about a week when she got sick. And I was 53 years, 5 months and about a week when the bus struck. And the amazing thing, besides the fact I survived, was that I didn't have a seatbelt and I didn't go through the windshield. No brain injury."

"Mom—unreal!"

"My mother's brain was destroyed. She used to say she could endure just about anything, as long as she had the freedom of her mind. I can't begin to imagine not having the freedom of my mind."

"Your mind's in good shape, Mom. Soon your body will be back in good shape too."

Dan was permitted to stay with me. With the Nanchang hospital experience still fresh in my mind, I envisioned his needing to sleep on the floor. His being provided with a cot reminded me I was in Canada.

Sunday, February 20, 2005, 7:00 p.m.

Missing My Students

Today I found myself composing a letter to my students at HUST. I don't know if I'll do anything with it. It may be enough for me to imagine its being read later this month at the assembly to start the new term. When I mentioned this to a nurse, I started to cry. I shared it with Dan.

To All My Dear Students:

There are so many things I want to tell you as I lie here in this hospital bed in Canada. First, I am incredibly sad not to be with you this first day of the new term. I am, however, extraordinarily thankful to be alive. I think Jonathan has already told you what happened. There are no words to describe how grateful I am to him and to other wonderful people from HUST who helped me: Dr. Zhao, Mr. Sun and Miss Zhang.

I was only with you for a few months but can tell you truly: You are the best! You are all young people with good hearts and I believe in you. Please, will you promise me something? I want you to believe in yourselves too. I want you to focus on your strengths—your goodness, honesty, kindness, friendliness. I posted virtue charts in some of the classrooms. Study them. I want you to do good things for China and for the world.

Some of you have my e-mail address. Please share it and write to me. Now I want you to smile. You know 'Laoshu Ai Da Mi'? Well, I still want to learn all the words to that song. Will some of you send them to me in pinyin with an English translation? That would be wonderful.

I hope I can see you all again one day. I will always remember you.

Ramona

When I finished reading the letter out, Daniel said, "Mom, you'll go back to China. You just wait and see." Who knows, maybe I really will return. Time will tell.

Monday, February 21, 2005, 9 a.m.

Gentle Touch Dream

"Will someone please touch my foot? I need to feel some warmth in my foot. Oh, why won't any of you help me?! You have no idea how awful this is! Please...."

Then I feel tentative fingers touch and massage, oh so gently, my swollen foot and ankle. Life flickers in flesh I feared dead. Yeming clears his throat and asks, "Ramona, my father wants to know if his touch is too hard." Really? He is the one?

In disbelief I opened my eyes to discover it was my beloved son Daniel caressing my foot. He had removed the bandaging. It wasn't Mr. Zhang after all. "Oh Dan, I must have been dreaming."

Because of My Little Dream

I closed my eyes again and thought about Mr. Zhang, a man who extended himself to help me in the Nanchang Hospital. Remembering his kindness, I felt my heart soften. When he and I first met, I didn't know what to make of him. His decision to exclude me from the New Year's activities left me feeling hurt and alone in an upstairs room. He seemed a man caught up in his own worldly success. He'd become a somebody and wanted others to know it. He'd commissioned a conspicuous monument to honour the memory of his father and he'd also constructed the showiest and biggest building in the town.

In the hospital, the Mr. Zhang I saw was anything but egotistical. For three nights he slept on a floor, available at a moment's notice to help me. Without complaint he fed me, sat me up and lay me back down, and helped me on and off a bedpan. After he was robbed, he wouldn't eat until his daughter reminded him that as the head of the household he must set a good example for his family. When he readily complied, I saw a man not wanting to let his family down. Mr. Zhang and I began with judgements

49

limiting each other and parted with those judgements washed away. Barriers of language and tradition were also washed away.

The father of my friend did not, in fact, massage my foot but he did so in my dream. There we touched. That man, I realized, was not who I thought he was. Because of my little dream, I was able to see with my heart and appreciate Mr. Zhang in a new, larger way. Because of my little dream, I felt a wordless meeting of our hearts.

Special Young People

Something was still troubling my heart and it was something that happened when I first arrived back in Canada. Talking to Dan helped.

"When I arrived in Emergency, I didn't recognize your sister right away. She must have thought I was brain damaged."

"Mom, you were in shock."

"I guess. You know, she only got back from Costa Rica a day or two before me. She almost extended her stay. Am I glad she didn't!"

"You couldn't help it. Don't feel bad. Maybe it was too much for you to hope she'd be back."

"You may be right."

"You've got both of us here. Aaron would be too if Edmonton wasn't so far away. He phoned, right?"

"Yeah. He'll get time off work in two or three weeks and come to Ray's in the Okanagan after I'm discharged."

"Good."

"Did I tell you I'd be staying there? And get this, your uncle Ray's making his house wheelchair accessible before he comes to pick me up."

"Cool."

"The hardest part of living in China was missing you guys."

"I missed you too, Mom. Remember when I messed up and called you at 4 a.m.? You said it was okay."

"It was. You know, something just occurred to me. I missed the three of you so much and the three friends I've been telling you about in China are in their 20s, like you. Boy, girl, boy too. Aaron's my oldest and Yeming I met first. Anna's my second and only girl, and Eria I met next. You're my youngest, and last I met Haiwu."

"What do you make of that?"

"Not sure. I wasn't trying to fill any gap, at least not consciously. It was like a gentle magnet, drawing each of them to me or me to them. Becoming friends was easy, completely natural, like breathing."

"Sounds special."

"Yeah, and I told them about you. You know how Rebecca is looking after my e-mail? Well, she sent a message to Haiwu and Eria for me and I asked her to attach the photo she took of you and me yesterday."

"What about the third friend? What's his name again?"

"Yeming. He was in the accident too. I need a little more time to think about what to say to him. Here's my message to Haiwu and Eria."

From: Rebecca
To: xxx@yahoo.com, yyy@163.com.cn
Sent: Mon., February 21, 2005
Subject: A note from Ramona

My Dear Haiwu and Eria,

A quick message, my dears, to assure you I am receiving excellent care. Recovery will be long but I have wonderful family support, which will help me greatly. Please relax. I will heal. I promise I'll see you again, though not at your graduation.

Attached please see a photo of my son Dan with me in the hospital. He'll be here for a few days and is missing his university classes. He was even given a cot so he could sleep in this room. He plays his guitar, and I've been telling him lots about China and about you two.

Take care and know that I love you both.

Ramona xo

PS This is Ramona's sister, Rebecca. She tells me what to say and I type her messages to send to you. If you would like to send Ramona a message, please send it to my address and I'll print it to give it to her, as she is still in hospital.

Introducing My Young Friends

Wang Nian Zhi Jiao

The Friendship of Forgetting Age Difference

As I considered all I'd told Dan, I felt myself awash in a warm sea of memories—the South China Sea. Yeming, Eria and Haiwu. What karma brought them into my life and what past lives did we share? I loved their innocence, their intelligence and their desire to make the most of their lives. Wang nian zhi jiao absolutely fits with each of them.

Yeming

I met Yeming first. I cherish all the hours he and I spent together listening to music, talking, walking and travelling. I'm sorry for all the difficulties of the accident but they are part of the shared experience. I remember the evening in a Harbin restaurant in late December when he told me about chengyu (pronounced chung-yew) an old and special type of idiom or proverb from Chinese classic literature. Apparently there are thousands and many are associated with a story. He wrote down *wang nian zhi jiao* and told me, "It's when two people of different generations are drawn together in a close friendship. It's the friendship of forgetting age difference." I almost started to cry. Inside I asked, *Has anyone ever caressed my soul with satin before?*

Yeming and I met in late November at the Saturday conversation class I taught at the HIT Study Abroad Centre for master's students. Looking back, I think he may have been drawn to me right away. At the end of our first class, he asked me lots of questions about pronunciation. Students eager to learn have always brought me joy. He and his friend Wood then invited me to have dinner with them on campus. I wasn't hungry but figured, *Hey, technology students? Maybe they can help me buy speakers for my computer.* They did and from then on Yeming and I were buddies. Neither of us could possibly know what lay in store for us within three months' time.

Eria

Next, I met Eria. I'll always remember the day she walked into my life in mid-December, about three weeks after I met Yeming. I had just about finished helping one of my students with an assignment, when a young lady whirled into my HUST office and announced, "Do you mind if I just sit and listen? I've overheard you talking to your students in the hallway and I like your voice." Her manner, self-possessed and a little bold, charmed me right away. A fourth-year English major, fluent in Japanese as well as English and Mandarin, Eria (an "English" name we made up) was soon to graduate from HUST. We became friends "just like that."

Almost immediately I knew, "This is the person I want to travel with—Chinese, bilingual, smart, confident and fun." A five-week holiday was coming up with Spring Festival, also known as Chinese New Year, right in the middle. The last day of classes was January 22. Colleagues asked if I wanted to go to Thailand. "No, I want to see China." It was a good thing none of us went to Thailand, considering the tsunami (26 December 2004). Anyway, Eria and I did decide to travel together. She kept telling me about her friend Haiwu, soon to graduate from HUST too.

"Ramona, you'll like him. You want to know more about Chinese literature. Well, Haiwu's really the one to ask. He likes writing too, just like you. He's going home to a town near Xiamen for the holiday. His parents have already invited us. We can stay as long as we like and they'll provide meals. Our only expenses will be transportation. Really."

I was blown away. *I get to stay with a Chinese family? It's that easy?* I said yes. Eria said she'd only be staying a few days, which I figured meant I'd need to leave too. Immediately I began to imagine visiting Yeming and his family. Maybe they'd invite me. Jiangxi was the province next to Fujian where Haiwu's family lived. Wherever I went, I wanted to be with Chinese people who'd "take me under their wing." Immersion in Chinese culture with a bilingual friend appealed to me. If that didn't work out, Heather in Shanghai said I could stay with her. She'd be working but would have some time to spend with me.

As it turned out, Eria and I left Harbin by air on January 25. Eria was a born teacher! She taught me many Chinese expressions and their accompanying stories, along with lessons on beauty. She educated and entertained me at the same time.

"Ramona, in our classics we have the legendary 'Four Beauties.' You must know about them. They really lived. They helped emperors, so were clever and brave too. First, Xi Shi. Her beauty was so great she dazzled fish when she walked by. They forgot how to swim and sank. Then Wang Zhaojun. When she looked upwards, the birds fell out of the sky. When Diaochan looked at the moon it couldn't compete. It felt ashamed so hid behind the clouds. Yang Yu Huan was so beautiful that flowers became shy, so closed their petals. When we want to compliment a woman's beauty we say that she is like these four beauties."

According to tradition, I learned, beautiful Chinese women were tiny, their delicacy such that a breeze could just about blow them over. These women had faces oval-shaped like a duck's egg and lips small and cherry-like. Arched like "distant hills," their eyebrows needed to be pencilled in exceptionally thin. Of course, if looked at, these ladies needed to cast their eyes down demurely, and if they should happen to smile or giggle, they must cover their mouths. Showing their teeth was considered crass. I was smiling when Eria shared that gem, so I quickly covered my mouth, which made us both laugh. I'm glad Chinese women have evolved past all that.

I continue to smile as I recall the many other little things Eria taught me that she thought important. "Ramona, *xiao* means little and can be used affectionately too. *Ke ai de* means cute or sweet or lovely. Girlfriends say these to each other but not to boys. *Xiao* and *ke ai de* are words we use with children too. When a boy compliments a girl, she can tease him with *tao yan*, which means I don't like it but I don't hate it either." Privy to harmless youthful sweetness, I was happy.

I loved Eria for her practicality too, making sure first things got looked after first. For example, Haiwu was travelling all the way to Xiamen by train. Knowing we'd fly and arrive one or two days before Haiwu, Eria arranged for us to stay with another of her friends, a former classmate, Yi Min, a lovely young man. Eria also planned activities for us while he worked. I will never forget visiting Gulangyu the "Island of Pianos," off the coast of the Island of Xiamen. It is subtropical and gorgeous. I could go on and on about those two days! But, now it's Haiwu's turn to be introduced, along with his family.

Haiwu

Meeting Haiwu and his family I felt as though I'd come home. They embodied love, kindness, generosity and real-ness. They were salt of the earth good people, sunshine and warmth. Haiwu's grandmother was a little 85-year-old lady with a long cigarette and a big toothless smile. Already I am smiling.

One memory I did not write down at the time is especially sweet. I happened to walk into the living room to find Haiwu's mom dyeing her husband's hair black. They both looked up at me, surprised and embarrassed. As soon as I smiled back, it didn't matter that I'd intruded. They relaxed and smiled back. They'd been married for going on thirty years. Haiwu told me they're still in love and each other's best friend. I'm smiling all over, just thinking about them.

After three and a half days Eria returned to Harbin as she'd planned. I didn't need to worry about what to do next, as Haiwu and his parents asked me, "Please, will you stay longer?" We'd only just met but how could I say anything but yes? It was my dream come true being looked after and looked out for by a wonderful Chinese family, who also happened to like me. And to top it off, Haiwu was bilingual!

What can I say about Haiwu? I feel as comfortable with him as I do with my son, Daniel. He's easy-going, smart, sensitive, strong and open. Haiwu and I talked a lot. I thoroughly enjoyed hanging out with him and his buddies Afu and Xiaohui, also home for the upcoming Spring Festival. The four of us walked all over town. I laughed more than I have in ages. I said to them, as I had to Eria earlier, "But I'm so much older than you." Their simple response was, "You are one of us. We don't feel any age difference." *Wang nian zhi jiao*, the friendship of forgetting age difference.

Oh, I want to learn Chinese! That they even have such an expression right in their language (and everybody knows it) is beautiful. In Haiwu's hometown, I was immensely happy. Given what has happened since, I feel happy and sad to remember that.

Fate or Destiny

Wednesday, February 23, 2005, 3:30 p.m.

Invisible Forces

Did fate bring all these wonderful young Chinese people into my life or are they part of my destiny? Invisible forces seemed to be at work. "Fate" is neutral and impersonal, yet it still has a disturbing ring about something done to us beyond our control, like earthquakes and avalanches and head-on collisions. If I'm content to blow with the breeze through life, then I live at the mercy of fate. Unconsciousness is not my thing.

Destiny, on the other hand, sounds promising and personal, as though I have a say in determining it. If I have a goal, a *destination*, that I determine, then *destiny* is apt to be involved. (I bet those two words are connected.) I create a destiny by the way I consciously and constructively deal with whatever fate throws at me. It's an empowering thought.

I seem to be the kind of person that when I get something into my head that I want to do, no matter what it is, and I do what I can to make it happen, then God or Essence says, "Hey, let me help that come true!" I made China happen in my life. That was no easy feat. The voice in the wreckage told me the accident was part of something bigger involving me and China. I don't have to pay attention to that message but I want to. Would I ever have received it if the accident hadn't happened? I know one thing for sure—my life will be vastly better because of the accident than if it had never happened. I'll see to it, and I want the "better" to involve China. So what will I choose as a destiny? Mmm... there's no hurry. The answer will come.

Yuan Fen

Haiwu taught me some thought-provoking idioms, again with no English equivalent. He said, "*Yuan fen* is when two people are meant to meet in a very meaningful way. Sometimes it's a close friendship, and sometimes it's a romantic relationship.

Circumstances work out for them and they are also diligent in working out any problems. They are happy and they're the lucky ones. When it's a friendship, we more often say the two people *you yuan* (have *yuan*), which is a special kind of luck."

Fate or destiny? It sounds as though the two friends or lovers play a key role in their own success. My three young friends and I must "have *yuan.*" (*You yuan* sounds a bit like *yo-yu'en*.) How, otherwise, could we have become good friends so easily and so fast? Maybe part of it has to do with our knowing how to be outgoing and bold rather than hesitant in pursuing what we want to have happen.

Haiwu told me, "*You yuan wu fen*, Ramona, is not so happy. It's only used with the romantic kind. The two people have the good fortune to meet and fall in love but it doesn't work out." I guess that's something most people have some experience with. It was plenty for me to think about.

Communication from China

Thursday, February 24, 2005, 10:30 a.m.

Remember the Phoenix Dream
When I awoke this morning my pillow was wet with tears.

Over and over I heard Haiwu's voice, "Ramona, remember the phoenix, remember the phoenix. Its burning is for good. Remember."

I lay here asking, *Why is he speaking of fire? Why this message?* Then I thought about the fire raging in my body: in my chest, elbow, right leg, knee, and my poor tummy. I cry the most for the pain in my tummy. What does the burning in my body have to do with the phoenix? Somehow I know this is what Haiwu meant. He wasn't saying I will have the burning in my body for good (forever); rather, the burning will be for my good.

Correspondence
My son left today. What a gift he is to me. I will miss him but not for too long. When I'm out of here and Dan's finished classes in April, he'll come to see me in the Okanagan. Before he left, I showed him Haiwu's and Eria's replies to my e-mail. My spirits lift with their encouragement and even more so when I share their messages with Dan. This first email is from Haiwu.

To: Rebecca
From: xxx@yahoo.com.cn
Sent: February 23, 2005
Subject: To Ramona Please

Dear Ramona:

I'm so glad to know that you have received better medical treatment. I see the photo, so I can totally relax now. Eria can see the photo too.

Please just take care of yourself and don't worry too much, because so many people care about you, love you. I still remember the words you told me. Now I want to tell you, my dearest friend, you are also the most beautiful person I have known. When you feel depress or not so good, just think of the words "You are the best."

I can't wait until I will meet you again in China. When this day comes, I can't be much happier and we can do lots of things together.

I'll be busy these days, because I have to prepare the important exam and find the job I like.

Say hello to Dan!
Recover soon!

Yours, Haiwu

Looking next at Eria's e-mail, I can't help smiling at some of the little imperfections. I hate to think of the faux pas I make when I attempt Mandarin. Her asking if I can understand her meaning is endearing. So many young Chinese say something and then look at me with earnest eyes and ask, "Can you understand my meaning?" It softens me every time.

From: yyy@163.com
To: Rebecca
Sent: February 23, 2005
Subject: Re: A note from Ramona

Hi, xiao Ramona,

I'm very glad to know that you are getting good care and it comfort me a lot on seeing your photo with Dan. I can tell you are feeling better through your smell [she means smile] although you still look tired.

I was greatly shocked after knowing your statement of leaving China. It's really a miracle that you can survive through all of it. I begin to believe that there is really some God in this world who is blessing good people.

But, I hope that God can be more kind and never allow you to meet any pain again because you are such an easy going person and you can always bring lots of happinesses to your friends. It would be unfair for you to suffer any more pain!

Dear, we went to the biggest temple here to pray for you last week, and we all wish you can be well soon. Haiwu will look for a job in other cities and I wish him good luck too.

A special message for you 'Dong tian guo qu le.' It means winter has gone away. Xiao Ramona, I wish your winter is all past. Can you understand my meaning?

By the way, it's not very clever for you to tire yourself now, take care and guaiguai de. All my best to you, your son and your family too. Remember your Chinese, our ke ai de xiao Ramona!

May God bless you,

Eria

Thursday, February 24, 2005, 8:11 p.m.

I have exchanged emails with Yeming now. I decided not to tell him the real extent of my injuries. Not yet. He replied quickly. I am relieved to know he and Haiming are fine. First, here's what I had Rebecca send him.

To: zzz@yahoo.com.cn
Sent: Monday, February 21, 2005
Subject: This is Ramona's Sister

I am Rebecca, Ramona's sister, and she has asked me to send this message to you as she is still in hospital. Please send your reply to me and I will give it to her.

My Dear Yeming,

I am thinking about you every day and I hope you are well. I hope you did not return to Harbin too quickly. Please do not worry about me. I want to assure you I am fine. I will recover and I will walk again. I am in a good hospital with good doctors and nurses. My family is also helping me greatly, so I am a very lucky person. (Please see the attached picture of me with my son who's staying with me for a while here.) Not only that, I will dance again. The party in your family's new home I will never forget. I was very happy. Please say "hi" to all your wonderful cousins for me.

Yeming, I hope you are being very kind to yourself. Remember what I said to you in the hospital? I asked you to promise me that you will never blame yourself for my injuries. We were both hurt and it was an accident. You have only ever been a wonderful friend to me. You have taught me so many beautiful things about China, and for that I will always be grateful. There is something very special about you, my dear friend, and I want to tell you. You are a person studying technology (which can be so impersonal), but you have a beautiful, sensitive and poetic soul. I never want you to lose this.

How is Haiming? I think about him often. A broken pelvis is a serious injury. Will he be able to walk again? Wish him good luck from me.

Please give my kindest regards to your family.

Take very good care of yourself.

Your friend,

Ramona

From: zzz@yahoo.com.cn
To: Rebecca
Sent: Wednesday, February 23, 2005
Subject: Re: This is Ramona's Sister

Hi Ramona,

First of all, let me say I felt your kindness as soon as I read your letter. It's so difficult to find English words to express my emotion and thought. You look happy in the picture to be with your son.

My family is very sorry for what happened to you. My mother has much worry. We want to know can you move your right leg yet? Does it feel painful? Will you be able to walk like before being injured? They said you were very optimistic even if the pain of your leg was awful. All of them admire you for your courage. And I'm proud of you, Ramona.

I remember the song you taught me—"It's raining, it's pouring, old man is snoring......couldn't get up in the morning." I can sing the song when it rains. And it reminds me of the happy time we spent in Jingdezhen. So you're my "wang nian zhi jiao"—this comes from my heart, not from my head.

Don't worry about my cousin Haiming. He is getting well. You ask me "Will he be able to walk?" That is for sure!

I am fine. After you left, I returned to Harbin and wrote the exam. For internship I tried for Canada but no luck. It looks like I will go to Lodz in Poland.

I am so sorry for your injury. I think I will pay you back to do something for you.

Always your friend,

Yeming

Back to a Time of Happiness

Oh, dear life, take me back to happiness, take me back to the first day of my wonderful trip, take me back to Xiamen.

Xiamen—Clean, Quiet and Beautiful

In Harbin, when I first heard mention of our upcoming winter holiday in January, I was excited. It would be a long one—five weeks—and Spring Festival would be in the middle of it. Ha! I remember Yeming smiling and calling me *jiao hua* (a tricky teacher) when I told him about the writing assignment I gave my students: "Plan a trip for me in China." Then I befriended Eria and she invited me to travel with her to Xiamen.

On January 25, such a short time ago, Eria and I left Harbin where the temperature was minus 20 degrees Celsius. We stopped twice, landing in Qingdao, a city famous for beer, and Wenzhou. In the clear weather I could see cities and fields far below us. I kept my China map open on my lap, eager to identify cities if I could. As we approached our destination, I could see the big island of Taiwan across the strait. It was a balmy 22 degrees when we arrived in beautiful, clean Xiamen, a subtropical island city in Southern China. Yi Min, Eria's friend, met us and we spent the evening together before sleeping at his place.

Moonlight Radiance

I can still savour the sensuous warmth and radiance of my first evening in Southern China. It must have been the same kind of evening that inspired the Chinese poets of old to write their eloquent verses. Under a shimmering full moon, Eria, Yi Min and I lay down on the soft grass by a lake on the campus of Xiamen University. As we looked up at the sky, Eria talked about the legend of the beautiful goddess named Chang'e, who lives in the moon. Once an earthly mortal, Chang'e found and swallowed a pill of immortality. She floated upwards and landed on the moon, where she became a goddess.

Once a year, Chinese people celebrate the Moon Festival and they tell their children the story of Chang'e. Also, if a girl is beautiful, people can say, *"Chang'e xia fan,"* which means the goddess has returned to earth.

The Melt Factor

Then Eria talked about a famous poem written almost 1,000 years ago by Su Shi, on a full moon night like this, I'm sure. The poem was made into a song—*Dan Yuan Ren Chang Jiu*, "May All My Friends Live Forever." Eria said Deng Lijun (Teresa Teng) sang it. The poet/writer, alone and far from home, raises his wine glass to toast the moon. Then, bathed in moonlight, he dances with his shadow. He misses his family and friends greatly and says something to the effect: "Though a thousand miles may part us, nothing can separate our hearts. We can be united tonight in sharing the beauty of this moon." I bet these lines are exquisite in the original Chinese. I could feel myself just about melt into the soft grass. When I hear the song, will I melt all over again?

From Xiamen University, we made our way to the sea over an amazing pedestrian overpass. The architectural design intrigued me and the walking surface felt like texturized rubber. With each step, I noticed its give, an ever-so-slight spring. I liked the feel. Yi Min explained the foot bridge was composed of recycled plastic from water and pop bottles.

I shall never forget walking along the shore and receiving a text message from Yeming in Jiangxi Province. "Where are you now, Ramona? I've just arrived home." With veritable happiness I floated on a cloud in a starry sky.

Island of Pianos

On our first full day, Eria and I decided to take a five-minute ferry ride from Xiamen to a pretty little island called Gulangyu (sounds like Goo-long-yew). It was magical. I felt as though I'd stepped back in time, perhaps into Renaissance Europe but in a subtropical setting with Chinese people and a twentieth-century Western presence. Fittingly, there were no cars on Gulangyu. We walked a lot, up and down. Walls topped with fancy stonework lined twisty, narrow, steep streets. Other streets had houses on either side, their doors opening right onto the street. It was my picture of a Renaissance Italian town. We saw old mansions, old foreign consulates and old churches. Some of these buildings were crumbling and ivy-covered, some had well-kept gardens, and some had unkempt gardens. I loved the sumptuous green and the flowers growing wild, some in crevices in stone walls. The past was very present.

We expected to hear piano music. We heard none but did hear a violin from a private home. Before returning to Xiamen, we sat on a beautiful sandy beach with palm trees. I never knew such a lush and lovely place as this existed in China.

The next day, I finally met Haiwu. He'd taken a train all the way from Harbin and had to stand the whole way from Beijing to Xiamen, more than thirty hours—unbelievable! I asked him what that was like. "Sleeping standing up is a little difficult but it's okay if it means going home for Spring Festival," he answered.

The first thing we did was go to the home of his aunt to leave all our travel bags. Later in the day we'd head to Haiwu's home an hour away from Xiamen. Until then, Haiwu's cousin, a 10-year-old boy, was happy to join us.

The four of us—Haiwu, his cousin, Eria and I—enjoyed a fabulous day of sunshine, friendship and fun, which included visiting and exploring the Nanputuo Buddhist temple. A sign near the entrance reminded us to "Conscientiously keep clean and pure the environment of the temple." Another sign read to "Cherish the flowers and the grass." I liked these and the many other little signs such as these we encountered in Chinese and in English.

The term *temple* refers to its many pagodas, monks' quarters, courtyards, gardens, terraces, pools and grottoes. The place was gorgeous! It's no wonder tourists love to visit. Built on the side of a lushly treed hill, it looks out over the ocean. Haiwu was pleased to be my guide and teacher. It turned out the things I expressly wanted to know about were the things he found important to tell me. He and I were on the same wave length.

The Nanputuo temple was first built in the Tang Dynasty in the A.D. 800s, and Haiwu explained it's not only a place of worship but also a training college for monks. Statues to represent the Buddha were of course plentiful. I was pleased to see many of Guanyin as well, the *Goddess of Mercy*. Some people say she is the female Buddha. From my understanding of the Catholic Church's view of Mother Mary, she and Guanyin are similar, both representing all the strength and goodness of the feminine or yin energy.

Xi Xin, Wash Your Heart

We climbed a great deal, up pathways irregularly lined with boulders, each with characters deeply engraved in its surface. Someone had painted each of the characters red. We found other large ancient stones in ponds.

One stone compelled my attention. The first of its two characters I'd already seen many times. It looked something like an "L" with three rain drops or tear drops. Haiwu told me it was *xin*—pronounced a bit like *sheen*.

"This word means 'heart,' Ramona, but more than that. I don't think there's an equivalent word in English. *Xin* also means 'mind' but a special kind of mind. It's not the mind that thinks in a regular manner. It's the mind of the heart."

"You mean like the knowing of the heart. The wisdom of the heart?"

"Yes."

"Haiwu, I love this word already. No wonder I was drawn to its character."

"The second character is *xi*. It means to 'wash or cleanse.' Here it also means to 'purify.' In olden times, Chinese was read from right to left, so *xin xi* is actually *xi xin* and means 'wash your heart.' In Buddhism it is important to clean the bad things from the heart so the goodness can come out."

"Shee sheen?"

"Almost. Another time I will teach you how to say our x sound correctly." Haiwu smiled at me. His obvious love of his language and culture appealed to me immensely.

We climbed up to a high look-out, where I could see Xiamen University buildings and gardens below. In the distance, the city glistened in the sunlight and ships sailed the strait between Xiamen and Taiwan. I lifted my chin, let the breeze blow my long hair all over the place, threw my arms wide and skyward and said, "Yes!" My friends smiled. No explanation was necessary.

After making our way back down to sea level, we found a little restaurant where Eria bought us a Buddhist vegetarian lunch and then we meandered round the campus grounds of Xiamen University, closed for the holiday. It had been moonlight the night before and it was now daylight so I could see the pale pink stone and rounded archways of some of the older buildings with their pagoda-style roofing. The fancy architecture of newer buildings we could see too but that didn't interest me as much. A pathway led us to and around a lake, the one I lay beside the night before. Little arched bridges, flowers and what I can only describe as pretty trees added to the quality of softness I liked so much.

The Phoenix

Feng huang shu or phoenix tree is the official tree for the city of Xiamen so I learned. I wish I could see it in bloom in late spring with fiery orange and red flowers. Haiwu told us about the legend of a big flood in Xiamen. A phoenix came to the people, saved them and then died. In one legend it burns to nothing then rises from the flames, differing from the Western phoenix that arises from ashes. The key to that particular legend is the phoenix chooses to sacrifice itself to the flames in order to help humans. Is that element part of the Western story too?

Dragon and Phoenix, Emperor and Empress

Hearing that legend, I had to know more about the Chinese phoenix, *fenghuang* or *bu si niao* "can't die (immortal) bird." Both Haiwu and Eria told me that next to the dragon, the phoenix is the most important creature in Chinese mythology. Its meanings include ever-lasting love, peace and longevity. Originally androgynous, the bird symbolized the unity of opposites or yin yang: male (*feng*, a yang creature), and female (*huang*, a yin creature). The phoenix, then, was complete unto itself.

The dragon (*long*) has only ever represented yang, masculine energy. When the dragon was lucky enough to have the phoenix join him, the androgynous *it* (that is, the phoenix) became a *she*, relinquishing androgyny for powerful feminine energy. The dragon, Eria told me, came to represent the emperor himself and the phoenix, his wife. Together they were a powerful symbol for oneness. "In much Chinese art, you will see the dragon and the phoenix dancing together," Eria also told me.

Long Feng Cheng Xiang

At weddings, people bless the couple by hanging banners of a phoenix and dragon, along with the words *long feng cheng xiang*: "Dragon and phoenix together foretells very good fortune— longevity, happiness, peace, prosperity." Eria mentioned that *long feng cheng xiang* is a *chengyu*, the same kind of old Chinese idiom Yeming had already told me about. *Chengyu* intrigue me. I marvel at what they reveal about the cultural mindset. China has a long and rich history reflected in their language. We have no real equivalent to *chengyu* in English.

When we left the university, we rode by the sea on a bicycle built for four, something like a big golf cart only with pedals. We were like little kids for all the fun we had. By this time it was late afternoon and we needed to leave Xiamen for the one-hour bus ride to Haiwu's hometown of Chang Tai (Long Peace), also in lush Fujian Province.

Smashing Taxi Driver

We had two taxi experiences en route to Chang Tai that I won't forget. Arriving early at the bus station was a very good thing, as the poor taxi driver could not get his trunk unlocked to retrieve our bags. It was funny for a while, especially when he started kicking it. I had to both walk and look away, I was laughing so hard. It stopped being funny when he took a crowbar type contraption and started clobbering. Prying would not work either. After about 10-15 minutes, he asked Haiwu to go with him somewhere. When they finally returned, I noticed the trunk broken open and the lid held in place with a rope! We managed to catch our bus.

Muscle Power Taxi Driver

About an hour later, we arrived in Chang Tai. How we managed to travel the rest of the way to Haiwu's home with all our bags was astounding. Here we were, three full-sized adults, with a ton of stuff, and our taxi was a cart "motored" by one small, very strong cyclist. He hardly charged anything, the equivalent of about 75 cents. I wanted to give him extra but my friends said, "Don't." Tipping is not customary. I had a hard time with that but listened.

Family Love

It was Haiwu's first trip home in a year. He was very excited and especially looked forward to seeing his mother. Thinking about how emotional I'd get seeing my kids, I said, "Haiwu, you go on ahead of us."

He said, "No, just come."

I imagined reuniting with my sons, hugging, talking and their picking me up and whirling me around. With Haiwu and his family, there was no touching and almost no talking but they all beamed like crazy. The love in the air was palpable.

Haiwu's grandmother and I are chatting like old friends, except we're not using words.

Entering that home will remain one of the most unforgettable experiences of my life, the kind of experience impossible to put into words. I met Haiwu's mother, father, aunt and an incredibly old-looking grandmother, the oddest yet most endearing little woman I have ever met. Four feet something tall, she was wearing a black velvet hat and enormous black-framed glasses. In her mouth was a cigarette with half an inch of ash dangling from the end. She had no teeth, a big smile and a great eagerness to push food on us. I was barely in the door when she started handing me bananas, sugar canes and oranges, grinning the whole time. She was Haiwu's paternal grandmother and lived there, as sons are supposed to take care of their aged parents. Her husband, Haiwu's grandpa, lived with another son.

It was about 8:30 p.m. Haiwu's mom steered us into a room and served us supper, a dish with very fine noodles, soup, barbecued chicken and snow peas. She then walked out and closed the door. Was it so we could eat privately together? It seemed strange. After eating, the three of us talked. Eria told an old Chinese tale about adult children casting their aged mother out into the wilderness to die. Eria thought it was the story that made me cry but the story was only one factor. I hadn't seen my children for a long time and there I was in China with beautiful young people letting me into their lives.

The story sounded awful until Eria explained that its purpose was to teach young children a lesson. The kids witness the abandonment of their grandmother and when they grow up they start to do the same to their aged mother who protests. Whereupon the kids say, "Well, you taught us." The moral of the story is "Don't follow bad examples. Take care of your mother when she gets old." Your father too.

I went to bed that first night well past midnight. Mosquito netting surrounded the three-quarter sized bed and a sheet of pink silk covered a mattress not much softer than the floor. Tired, I lay awake, luxuriated in my day and basked in my growing appreciation and love for China. I hadn't met Haiwu before that day, yet already I knew I liked him very much.

I replayed our conversation from earlier in the day. "Ramona, I was raised in a Taoist household, my grandmother is a Buddhist, and at university I was introduced to Christianity. All three belief systems have shaped me." I could relate. I told him that the label "Christian" no longer fits but the spirit of that religion still lives in me. I know both Old and New Testaments but I turn to the *I Ching* (Taoist *Book of Changes*) for guidance and support. I subscribe to the Buddhist precepts of right action, right thought and right speech. I try to be mindful of being mindful and I believe in reincarnation. Smiling, I could imagine the conversations in store for Haiwu and me.

I also considered my extraordinary good fortune. I was living a dream from my childhood to sojourn in a foreign land and immerse myself in its intriguing culture. The bonuses were that I was able to communicate more deeply with educated people of that land. Beautiful young Chinese had invited me into their hearts and a wonderful Chinese family had welcomed me into their home. I felt loved, valued and cared for. It was an experience beyond anything I had imagined.

Friday, January 28, 2005, 9:45 p.m. Chang Tai, Fujian Province, PRC

Joy

I am so happy I think my heart will burst! I have never before felt quite like this. I am blessed with three young Chinese friends, Eria, Haiwu and Yeming, and I love them for the dear people they are.

This evening Haiwu said to me, "You bring so much happiness to all my family and to my hometown. My family thanks you for coming here. My hometown thanks you for coming here."

I was overwhelmed. He was expressing exactly what I felt but the other way round. I said, "I thank your family. I thank your hometown. You all bring me happiness." What else could I say?

Yes

We've been in Fujian Province for three days (one full day in Xiamen/Gulangyu and two here in Chang Tai). Eria will be leaving in a couple of days. Even before coming, I knew she'd be heading back to Harbin before the end of the month. I thought it was unlikely I'd get to see Yeming so I'd just head to Shanghai, but that's all changed now! Haiwu and his family have asked me to stay on and I have said yes. With all the laughter and love, it was an easy decision to make.

Then the most wonderful thing happened. Yeming phoned to say his parents are inviting me to celebrate Spring Festival with them in about a week's time. I will stay with Haiwu and his family in Chang Tai, Fujian Province for about another week and then take a train to meet Yeming and his family in neighbouring Jiangxi Province. Yeming can meet me on Sunday, February 6 in Jingdezhen. Apparently it's a 19-20 hour train trip.

Getting a ticket for travel at this time of the year is tricky. Late this afternoon Haiwu and Eria took me to the station, far from town, to check on that possibility. The station master said to call tomorrow at 9 a.m. Here's hoping.

Train Ticket

I was successful the next morning due to the advocacy of one very persistent young woman named Eria, who managed to have me deemed a "VIP." Translation: the only way I could get a train ticket. It reminded me of when I was in Harbin. My being a VIP *wai jiao* (foreign teacher) certainly helped me and some of my Chinese friends there.

The ticket I managed to acquire was for a soft sleeper. For some reason this ticket was for Huangshan (Yellow Mountain), a city past Jingdezhen in Anhui Province. I could still disembark at Jingdezhen, of course. I had to pay the extra difference for the farther city. Fine by me. The grand total was only 337 rmb, about $50. Cheap. I'd be leaving Chang Tai, Fujian Province, at 10:20 a.m. Saturday, February 5 and arriving in Jingdezhen, Jiangxi Province at 5:30 a.m. Sunday, February 6. Before then, I still had many days to enjoy in Haiwu's childhood home, an hour from the coast in Fujian Province.

Before Eria left, she, Haiwu and I visited his parents' farm. It didn't produce all the family income, as his mom worked full time as a cleaner at the hospital. His dad had some kind of business. Their industriousness was pretty obvious. Their home had two stories and potential for a third. Haiwu explained that a third would give them much higher social status but they had used that money to support his education instead. I also learned that the house was built of concrete to withstand typhoons.

Paternal Grandfather

Eria was eager to meet Haiwu's grandfather and we did that too. We visited the elderly gentleman where he lived in his other son's home and in his own way he was just as sweet-looking as his wife. His white hair was combed back, he had a wispy beard and wore a black leather jacket. He didn't really say anything. His father or grandfather was the town chief and an important official. Before the Communist Revolution, Haiwu's grandpa was a landlord. Haiwu knew little about his background. If I could speak Chinese, I'd want to ask the old fellow a million questions. I thought of the amazing stories I'm sure he could tell, some very painful is my guess.

Eria and Haiwu with his grandfather

Nurturance: Loving Care and Chinese Medicine

Eria left and I stayed with people I'd only just met. Looking back, I can see more clearly what a nurturing time Chang Tai was for me. I was tired and my throat started to hurt shortly after arriving. I told Haiwu how hard I'd been working for a long time. He said, "There's nothing either of us needs to do. I want you to rest." I took his advice. With roosters crowing all day (all night too—heaven knows why they do that), cats in heat and women scrubbing their laundry outside, I didn't get "untired" but I did relax.

When Haiwu's mom saw me rubbing my right wrist and

heard that I'd broken it just before coming to China, she knew exactly what to do. With some healthy-smelling Chinese liquid stuff to aid circulation, she vigorously massaged my wrist for about thirty minutes. Then she applied some Chinese medicinal bandage-type things called "strengthen bone moschus analgesic plaster." Several times afterward, she did the same and it made a difference. A woman who'd never gone to school and was unable to read or write helped me more than both the hospital doctors I saw in Harbin. She showed me some exercises too and smiled the entire time. I liked her and Haiwu's father very much and I didn't even know their names. I decided to think of her as *Ke ai de*, Lovely.

Ke ai de was a sweetheart in other ways too. She was a born care-giver. After I showered one day (they had hot running water), she combed and blow-dried my hair. Hearing about my sore throat, she supplied me with Chinese cold medication.

Wo Bao Le

As for her meals, Ke ai de used only the freshest of food. One day I saw her on their doorstep slitting the throat of the chicken she cooked for supper that night. There was a bowl to catch the blood. Haiwu was in heaven with all the tasty home cooking. His mother's creed, much like my Italian grandmother's, seemed to be "food is love." Due to abdominal problems, I often wanted little or nothing. Ke ai de didn't ask; she just kept filling my bowl up. I didn't want to offend her by refusing, especially given possible cultural differences I didn't know about. I eventually grumbled at Haiwu, who thought the matter funny.

"No, really, Haiwu, how do I deal with this?!"

"Turn your bowl over and say '*bao le.*' That means 'I'm full.'"

When I did as he said ("bao" rhymes with "cow"), it helped a bit. Those times, I got away with eating less and only vegetables. The food issue tied in with bathroom problems. What I really needed to do was get over my pride and ask for a laxative.

Ke ai de would gladly have provided me with something. It also would have been helpful if I'd figured out much earlier how to flush their squat toilet. Too much pride to ask got in my way there too.

When Eria phoned from Harbin, she asked,

"Does Haiwu's mom still want you to eat and eat and eat?"

"Yes, yes, yes."

"Can Haiwu do something to help?"

"Yeah, he told me how to say 'I'm full' and turn my bowl over. I'm trying. Even when I do that, she still wants me to eat. For example, last night."

"What happened?"

"It was late, and I was just about asleep. Suddenly the light came on. She walked in with a bowl of hot soup and left. I've had a sore throat and I know she meant to be kind."

"What did you do?"

"I drank the broth and left the rest. She gave me an odd look this morning. I feel kind of bad but not that bad. I need to look after myself."

Even though my abdominal issue probably played a part in my horrible tummy problem now, back here in Canada, my time spent in Chang Tai had been very good for me, mostly because of Haiwu. We walked and talked a lot. One afternoon in the city's south Taoist temple, we sat and opened our hearts. As his confidante, I felt honoured by his trust.

He may have felt the same when I shared my work-too-much life in Canada and in China. My fatigue. My loneliness. The empty feeling of returning to an empty home. How much I missed my kids. Haiwu listened. I don't cry easily with other people but there was no way I could hold in those tears. Finally, when we walked back to his home I told him, "The girl who marries you will be lucky and she'd better think so too!" I was also able to say, "There are three young people in China I love so much—you, Eria and Yeming." With Haiwu, my heart has a way of growing big.

Three Handsome Dudes, Four Gentlemen and One American

Tuesday, February 1, 2005, 9:41 p.m. Chang Tai

Three Handsome Dudes

This morning Haiwu and I went shopping with his childhood buddies who are also home for the holidays, Afu and Xiaohui. Awesome young men! Afu will soon be graduating with a degree in computer engineering from a military university in Changsha in Hunan Province. He plans to continue in a master's program and talks about coming to Canada for his PhD. Xiaohui will graduate soon in electrical engineering from Fuzhou University in Fujian Province's capital city.

The calibre of so many of the young people I meet in China, including my HIT students in Harbin, is impressive not just for their brilliance but their character too. I consider myself very fortunate to have them in my life. We walked around town and enjoyed a lot of good-natured fun. I bought us some local oranges, the best oranges I have ever tasted.

Four Gentlemen
A Lesson on Flowers and Bamboo

I wanted to stop at the big flower market just to look around. I asked the guys if China had a national flower. They didn't think so but said, "We have the Four Gentlemen, *mei lan zhu ju.*" Oh? Something about four particular plants, super famous in China, that personify four or more traits that the "ideal person" has, according to Confucius. I love it!

Mei lan zhu ju is a *chengyu*, that special kind of idiom Yeming taught me about in Harbin. Each of the four words of *mei lan zhu ju* refers to a different plant. *Mei hua* (plum blossoms), *lan hua* (orchids), *zhu* (bamboo), and *ju hua* (chrysanthemums). Hua means flower or flowers. All four have been idealized in poetry and classic art.

I was a bit surprised about the chrysanthemums but shouldn't have been, considering how many I saw in Harbin. Anyway, chrysanthemums bloom late in the year and stay colourful and strong even in the face of cold winds and early snow. Plum flowers are red and they bloom at the beginning of the year in even colder weather. Even though plum blossoms look delicate and fragile, they withstand brutal weather conditions and never fail to return the following year. These two flowers symbolize courage, strength, perseverance, resilience, beauty and hope. Being colourful during dismal times indicates optimistic people who can encourage others. This all sounds so Chinese to me.

As for bamboo, I love that plant, so graceful and proud. Maybe I can go to Sichuan Province one day or the right areas of this province and walk through bamboo groves. It's very versatile in its usefulness, my young friends emphasized, and it's strong, withstanding vicious wind storms. After the storm has passed, bamboo straightens itself up again to stand tall. Its symbolism is resilience, flexibility, usefulness and an upright character. We talked about its hollow centre. What we came up with was an open heart and an uncluttered mind, the "superior individual." How refreshing. I had initially been stuck in Western negative associations with the word *hollow*.

The orchids referred to are the kind that grow or used to grow wild and fragrant in shadowy wooded areas in Southern China. They symbolize both integrity and an educated individual of noble character, or *junzi*, Confucius's ideal person. As is apparent, the Chinese have bestowed many anthropomorphic qualities upon the natural world. Their traditional culture's clear affinity with nature resonates with me.

I told the young men I always associate jasmine with China. They said it really isn't considered special. It has fame only because of the song *"Mo Li Hua."* They figured I must have already heard it. I'm not sure. I look forward to finding out.

Little Language Lesson

Haiwu, Afu and Xiaohui gave me a lesson on how to pronounce the "x" sound. It's not actually the same as "sh" though it's similar. So the word *xiang* (think) is not "shee-ong." I need to press my tongue lightly against my bottom front teeth, make my lips into a smile and "try" to say "shee" but of course it comes out a bit different than if I were just saying the sound "shee" in English.

One expression, not with an "x" but with a "z," I learned quickly today, that is, without their needing to repeat it—*you ba*. Sounds like "zoh-bah," with the stress on the second syllable. It means, "Let's go!"

I shared what a godsend pinyin is for me. To be able to read Chinese sounds in my own alphabet means there's some hope of my learning Chinese! As for the four tones in Mandarin, there are markers in the pinyin. Given my Western ears' inability to distinguish one tone from the other, the markers should help.

One American

As we walked back to Haiwu's, I heard a male voice boom from across the street, obviously addressing me. "Hey, whereya from?" I looked over to see a blond Caucasian fellow on a motorcycle, engine still running, with his Chinese wife seated behind him. I'm glad he called out or I would not have seen him. His name was Tim, from Bethel, New York, and he's been in China for eight years. His wife's Mei Li, which means 'Beautiful' in English. Tim teaches conversational English at Xiamen University.

Haiwu said, "Come to lunch." They were happy to accept the invitation and Haiwu's mom was even happier to feed a whole gang.

After lunch, Mei Li went shopping and the young men and I all went to Tim and Mei Li's place. One by one Tim taxied us on his motor bike up some big hills. He and Mei Li apparently have a place in Xiamen as well. Their home here in Chang Tai is lovely. Tim put an American movie into their DVD player and turned on their huge TV, not that any of us were in the mood for that. Tim was far more interesting.

I was able to make suggestions for his upcoming classes, which he seemed to value. I mentioned how I feel self-conscious taking Chinese people's pictures when I'm out and about, without their permission. Tim said, "Heck, do it anyway. They don't care about getting your permission." I know.

He then told me an interesting story. One day someone he didn't know walked into his class unannounced and took a picture of him teaching. Later Tim saw his picture used in an ad for a language school in Xiamen with a blurb saying, "Study English conversation classes with a native English speaker," namely Tim.

"What happens when students sign up and neither you nor any other 'native English speaker' is the instructor?" I asked.

"They just say something like 'Oh, that teacher? He got called back to the States at the last minute.' Students who paid their money can be pissed but what can they do?"

"I've had lots of people take my picture openly and not so openly but never in my classroom."

"Yeah, so don't feel bad about taking theirs," Tim said.

"A lot of times when I'm out, my friends tell me, 'They're talking about you.' I ask, 'What are they saying?' 'That your eyes are beautiful.'"

"Chinese girls like Westerners' eyes. Some even spend a ton of money on cosmetic surgery." Saying that, Tim shrugged his shoulders. My sentiment exactly.

Mountain Duck

Tomorrow Tim and Mei Li will pick Haiwu and me up in their jeep and take us somewhere "wonderful" about an hour from here, "in the mountains." Unfortunately Afu and Xiaohui can't come as there isn't enough room. Mei Li knows people there and wants to buy one of their ducks. She figures ducks from the mountains "taste better" than other ducks. As for me, duck is yuck—way too rich and greasy.

Yes, an adventure with nice people! I can't remember the last time I have felt so much happiness. Maybe never. Although I still have a sore-ish throat, my heart is full.

Wednesday, February 2, 2005, 10:18 p.m.

Backwoods of Fujian Province

Or should I say "back mountains?" It was a cool day. At about 10 a.m., Tim and Mei Li picked us up in their jeep. We drove into the mountains where a 4 X 4 is definitely needed. Up and up we went, stopping every now and then. We encountered nose-ringed water buffalo and people on bicycles loaded with green bananas. I saw mud brick houses, some with roofs of corrugated metal. I wondered how those houses fare in a typhoon or maybe that's a non-issue. At one place villagers, including lots of kids, were packing something called Fujian jujubes into crates. It was apparently a highly prized and delectable fruit that's used in some traditional Chinese medicines. It would be interesting to know what kind of ailments Fujian jujubes help to remedy. I didn't think to ask.

In the jujube place Tim had a great time teasing and rough-housing with the kids. Later, where women were cutting sugar cane with machetes, the road was blocked temporarily to load the tops onto a wagon, maybe for animal feed. Since we had to wait anyway, Tim struck up a conversation with a serious-looking older man. The man gave me the most wonderful smile when I indicated I'd like to take his picture. It was like the sun coming out from behind grey clouds!

Man with the beautiful smile in a Fujian sugar cane field.

89

I felt privileged to be in this out-of-the way place, amidst hard-working people focused on their tasks. Come to think of it, I don't think I have ever met a Chinese person who is not hard-working.

If Terraces Could Talk, What Tales Would They Tell?

We arrived at our destination, a remote small village. Tim and I walked up beside the terraces, which looked unplanted. I couldn't help wondering if tea had been grown in this place at one time. Tim told me he'd heard tell of warlords hiding out in these mountains and of fortunes' worth of American dollars still stashed in caves—money paid by the US government to support the Kuomintang back in China's Civil War days. If these terraces could talk, what tales of intrigue might they tell?

Mei Li's friends were very nice and served us bowls of noodles outside around a little fire. It was chilly up there. I walked among the ducks and came close to a nose-ringed water buffalo. The "lavatory" was up a trail beside the pigs and kind of gucky but private. Just before we left, Mei Li got her duck (poor thing), which was unceremoniously shoved, flapping, into a sack.

We took a different route back to Chang Tai with more highway driving this time. Upon our return to Chang Tai, the first order of business was to take the duck to a butcher. Apparently, eating duck is far more common here than eating chicken. While we waited for the slaughter to happen indoors, I saw someone slit the throat of a goat outdoors at the side of the road. Before going home, Tim and Mei Li came back to Haiwu's for supper.

It's late. I'm mellow after a long, eventful, satisfying day. I had a hot shower and got myself doctored up with Chinese medicine to help vanquish the cold that seems to be brewing. Before he went to bed, Haiwu thanked me again. "It was because of you I went into the mountains." He'd never been before. I am very happy about that.

Thursday, February 3, 2005, 6:10 p.m. (chilly, wet day)

Ni Chi Le Ma?

Haiwu bought lots of ingredients for a hot pot and it was a drop-in affair all day. With one friend stopping by, then another, it was "eating time" all over again. Food really is a big deal here. *Ni chi le ma* (Have you eaten)? Yup, and it's time for more!

I have been here a full week. On Saturday morning I leave for the 19-hour train ride to Jingdezhen. I'm glad this has been a peaceful, lie-low kind of day. Tomorrow Haiwu and I will spend the day in Zhangzhou, a city that forms a triangle with Chang Tai and Xiamen. It's about an hour each way by bus. I'm sure we'll walk a lot and, among other things, we'll visit an impressive Buddhist temple. Lovely.

Ni Hen Hao

I finally know Haiwu's parents' names: his dad is A Zhao, meaning "the sun is shining." His mom is Lai Hua, a kind of beautiful tropical flower. For me, she's still Ke ai de. She and the grandma often look at me, smile, then say, *"Ni hen hao."* "You are good/kind/nice." When they say that, they are voicing my feelings about them exactly.

Liang Shi Yi You

Oh my, the sweetness of the Chinese language for sentiments of appreciation! I am blown away. What the Chinese express in four little *chengyu* characters requires several words in English. *"Liang shi yi you"* means "You are my good teacher, my mentor and my dear friend" all at the same time. A little while ago Haiwu told me, "I have learned more from you in the past few days than I have from all my Chinese English teachers in the past four years." He wasn't talking about grammar. He was talking about life.

In return I told him the expression "mutual admiration society," then said, most sincerely, "You are one of the most beautiful people I have ever met."

With Haiwu's mom (Ke ai de), dad, Haiwu and Xiaohui. On my wrist is some of the Chinese medicinal tape Ke ai de gave me.

That Little Thing Called Language

Language, the vehicle by which we communicate, fascinates me. Without it, could we really think much? Thousands of languages exist. Each has its own gaps, "the what's the word for 'no word for it?'" And each undoubtedly has words to fill in some of the others' gaps. Still, if it were possible to combine all languages into one, with all possible gaps filled in, would we be much further along? No. How could we be? Given all that there is beyond human capacity to imagine, our combination would clearly be lame and that's not even taking into account non-verbal language. All this is food for thought, which of course will be in language.

Thursday, February 3, 2005, 11:25 p.m.

A Jolly Visit!

This evening Haiwu and I walked a lot and many businesses were still open. It was funny meeting his little grandmother in town. She looked sheepish when we found out she'd gone out to buy cigarettes.

I stopped to watch a man pounding a freshly made quilt with a peculiar-looking contraption. He was not pounding so much as fluffing it up. He was very friendly, beaming when I wanted to take his photo. He then shut off his machine and invited us in for tea. It was a jolly little visit. His handsome son, a lawyer who was in the P.L.A. (People's Liberation Army) for thirteen years, joined us. The son's wife and 10-year-old daughter showed up after a while too. What a happy way to end our walk in town. And tomorrow is our big day. It's off to Zhangzhou we go!

Quilt maker in Chang Tai

Dragon Day

I will always remember the simply wonderful day Haiwu and I spent in Zhangzhou. But first, I want to mention the conversation during the bus ride. Although I'd heard a little about the dragon a few days before, I wanted to know more, so I asked Haiwu:

"What's so special about the dragon in China?"

"Dragon is king. He is powerful, wise, strong, brave and benevolent." Haiwu spoke with authority.

"Sounds something like our associations in the West with the lion, who's known to be courageous and magnanimous."

"Magnanimous?"

"Noble-spirited, generous, big-hearted. There was once an English king called 'Richard the Lion-Hearted.'"

"Okay, sounds similar. Some dragons control the weather, and many towns and cities have special dragon temples. Farmers from the countryside sometimes still pray there for rain at the right time."

"So Chinese dragons are good?"

"Yes. Chinese dragons are auspicious. They're magical. They bring blessings to the people. All Chinese people respect them."

"It's quite different in our mythology. In the West dragons are bad. They steal and hoard treasure in their caves, kidnap beautiful maidens, and breathe fire to burn down whole villages. Knights were supposed to go out to rescue maidens and slay dragons. I think they're also supposed to be smelly and kind of stupid."

"Ha ha! So they live in caves?"

"Yeah, in mountains and in the earth, and their element is fire. What about Chinese dragons?"

"They live in the clouds, in rivers and deep in the sea, sometimes in crystal palaces. Their element is water. I'll tell you a famous *chengyu* later and its story."

White Jade Day

Our entire day in Zhangzhou was *haojile*, wonderful. I already called it a "Dragon Day." Looking back, I now want to call it a "White Jade Day" too. (I made up those expressions for myself to mean an awesome day.) I don't know if white jade is actually more special than other kinds of jade or not. I'd just never seen it before so it seemed extra beautiful. In the Buddhist temple we saw a lot of both white and green jade, a gem highly prized by the

94

Chinese. I have always loved this stone, so I'm in good company.

Haiwu told me jade was the "Stone of Heaven" that the "Sons of Heaven" (the emperors) treasured. When they died, they had their bodies shrouded in jade body suits held together with gold wire, the heavenly stone ensuring immortality. Many additional items made from jade were buried with them and other members of their royal families. People believed that in life, jade could both protect them from earthly harm and link them with the world of spirit. Oh, the amazing properties!

I once spoke with a Chinese man in Canada who told me his mom wore a heart-shaped jade pendant to protect her heart and soul. Lovely. And then there are the poetic descriptions in some of my *I Ching* commentaries, about jade's gentleness (softness and lustre) combining with jade's hardness (strength and durability) to make a gem pure and beautiful and tough.

Buddhist Temple

Meng li means "in my dreams." This little phrase could describe my experience at the Buddhist temple, where I felt as though I was walking in a dream of contentment. Standing alongside an incredibly long bas-relief wooden wall and then amidst both wooden and jade dragons and gods, I marvelled at the artisans' skill. The white jade, especially, glowed with a soft and lustrous sheen. The colourful altars, adorned with candles, fruit, incense and flowers (lilies, chrysanthemums, marigolds and roses), I found most pleasing too.

We happened to walk by the monks' canteen after they'd finished their lunch. A woman cleaning tables invited us in to eat whatever remaining food we wanted. It was a simple and nutritious lunch, free, courtesy of the temple.

Zhangzhou City

After spending two to three hours on the temple grounds, we walked over an old bridge with "speed bumps" that were actually blockades. Keeping vehicles off would help preserve the bridge for pedestrian traffic and/or for historical purposes. In the distance was a glitzy new bridge and directly in front of us were new apartment, office and business complexes. To the side, expanses of land levelled by bulldozers met our gaze.

We walked through a fascinating area where dozens of old homes and shops lay in ruin, the walls of brick and plaster still standing but the interiors gutted. A few people rummaged about. It was strange to see bits and pieces of china cups and bowls poking out of debris. I wondered who used to drink from those cups and eat from those bowls and what family stories lay destroyed in the dust. If I'd grown up here, would I feel deeply saddened or would I be excited, caught up in the frenzy of Old China's giving way to the New?

When Haiwu and I heard a chorus of "Happy Birthday" being sung (in Chinese of course) over the rubble, we realized that people still lived hereabouts. They obviously knew, all too well, the wrecking ball and bulldozers' imminent arrival to enforce their complete displacement. I mused, *Soon the unique, lively Chinese neighbourhood that once stood here will be flattened to nothingness, just like the other bare spaces close by. In no time, the emptiness will be filled with cookie-cutter-style apartments just like the thousands of other cookie-cutter-style apartments around here.*

Suddenly, echoing in my mind, I could hear my Harbin student Nancy's indignant remark, "China is not a Third World country. China is a developing nation!" I must have put my foot in my mouth. "Yes, I hear you, Nancy." Still, I couldn't help wondering: *Is China losing China?*

Haiwu and I next walked through another notable place in the downtown core. It was a historic neighbourhood with narrow streets, street vendors, little shops, motorbikes, bicycles, bicycle taxis and even the odd car. Browsing, I saw a lamp I was sorely tempted to buy, similar to those adorning the temple we'd just come from. Multiple "lotus flowers," each with its own teeny white, pink, blue, yellow or green bulb. "Very pretty, very colourful and far too impractical for me to buy as a traveller," I concluded as I left the store.

A sign saying "Zhangzhou Historical Neighborhood of Tang and Song Dynasties" listed the special structures the local district was intent upon preserving. These included the Ming Memorial Archway, Zhangzhou Confucius Temple, Wang Sheng Ancestral Temple, the former residence of the writer Yang Sao, the "ancestral residence of the descendants of the family surnamed Xu in Taiwan," and shops such as the "Heavenly Longevity Herbal Medicine Shop" and "Great Harmony" stationery store. It was a pocket preserved for posterity I'm glad to say.

From the historical area, we made our way past a McDonald's (how unfitting) to a huge city park with people of all ages taking in the sun. I smiled to see hundreds of old people obviously enjoying themselves. Some sat playing cards. Others chatted at little tables with their tiny cups and pots of tea kept warm by portable heaters. Many of the old men smoked cigarettes. We came across one delightful group of old fellows, each with a much older Chinese musical instrument, performing traditional songs. Finally I discovered the name of the instrument that makes the whiny kind of sound I go crazy over. It was an *erhu*, which two of the men played. I took a picture but now wish I'd made a little video.

Haiwu and I went into a CD-DVD store. Here I could buy knock-offs far more "professionally done" than those for sale on the street. I wonder how long it will be until the big crackdown, if there is one. I knew what I especially wanted, *The Wizard of Oz*. I'd re-watched the movie in Harbin, and it touched me all over again with its magic and love and innocence. I wanted to buy it to share with my friends later. I also wanted Teresa Teng CDs, and "Laoshu Ai Da Mi" ("Mice Love Rice"). Haiwu helped me find these and suggested many other CDs, which I bought. We finished shopping then headed for the bus to take us back to Chang Tai.

Musicians in a Zhangzhou city park

Bus Ride Back—Chengyu and a Dragon Story

On our way back, Haiwu and I talked more about dragons. I reminded him about his promise of a dragon story based on a *chengyu*. Here's the story he told me:

Hua Long Dian Jing

Once upon a time there was an artist named Zhang who painted people and animals so realistically that they came to life. His reputation caught the attention of the emperor himself who said, "I commission you to paint four dragons on a wall in my temple." So, Zhang painted four grand dragons to perfection, except that he omitted the pupils of their eyes. People came to see and were indeed awestruck, and puzzled too.

"Why didn't you finish their eyes?"

"If I did that they'd come alive."

"Ha ha," the people said, almost disbelieving him. "You're just making that up."

"You really want me to finish their eyes?"

"Uh... yes."

"All right, but you'd better brace yourselves."

As soon as he dotted the eyes, there was a mighty explosion. The roof burst open, and amidst thunder and lightning the dragons came to life and flew over the top of the temple, far away into the vast and stormy sky. The End.

I loved it! Haiwu explained once again that many *chengyu* come from the classics and they all have a meaning. Both Yeming and Eria had already taught me some. Everybody knows the meaning behind the most popular ones. *Hua long dian jing* means "paint dragons dot eyes" but the full meaning is "paint pictures of dragons and dot the pupils of their eyes." It signifies adding one little detail to an already really good creation and have it come to life. From good to "over the top," like those dragons.

Last Night in Chang Tai

When Haiwu and I got back in the early evening, his friends Afu and Xiaohui were waiting for us. Ke ai de happily served us supper then the four of us walked to the flower market (as though I hadn't already walked enough for one day). The next morning I was to start on my journey to visit Yeming and wanted a little gift for his family, something special for the Spring Festival. I'd heard that daffodils from southern Fujian Province were famous throughout the country. I found some bulbs with many sprouts that only needed placing in a bowl of water to bloom. Haiwu asked me what colours I liked. What a sweetheart! After I told him, he made a big bouquet of chrysanthemums and presented them to me.

I went to sleep that last night in Chang Tai present to goodness, my visit more wonderful than I could ever have imagined. I was full of hope for the continuance of my China travels.

The In-Between Time

Saturday, February 5, 2005, 10:34 a.m. Chang Tai train station

Happiness

I am sitting on the train, which is scheduled to leave at 10:51. Haiwu, Xiaohui and Afu came to see me off. Only Haiwu was permitted to come onto the train to help me. He had to pay 6 yuan, about $1, for that. When I said goodbye to his friends, there was much sweetness and warmth. We'd had a lot of fun together. Both expressed eagerness to stay in touch with me via e-mail, and Xiaohui, who knows much less English than Afu or Haiwu, earnestly told me he will improve his English so he can communicate with me better. I only shook their hands but really I wanted to hug them.

When Haiwu and I said goodbye on the train I had to fight against tears and managed to say, "I won't get emotional!"

That was good because he said, "Right. Our reunion will be soon." Yes, Harbin will come soon enough. After getting permission, I hugged him. Chinese people don't hug much. At least I haven't seen any Chinese people hug since arriving four months ago. It was as though I gave Haiwu the green light because he gave me the biggest hug I've probably ever had. I am happy. I've had a wonderful holiday so far with new, kind-hearted Chinese friends and I'm on my way to visit another friend. Dear God, how could I be anything but happy?

Saturday, February 5, 2005, 4:22 p.m.

The noise and sway of this train make me dopey. I slept little last night. I wish I could sleep now... I have a headache and a very heavy and sore abdomen. Ke ai de wanted to know what I wanted to take on this journey for food. I said, "Only a little fruit and some water." I am *not* happy or comfortable with the weight I've put on. Today I'd like to give my system a rest from food. Well, I easily have 15 pounds of fruit with me including oranges, apples, pears, bananas, and a huge grapefruit-like thing. I honestly do not know how she could think I'd eat even half! I may just leave most of it on the train.

I am in berth #31, compartment #8, and have what's called a "soft sleeper," meaning I'm in a compartment with three (actually four) others. A very pleasant army man, on his way home to Anhui Province, has just joined us. So, two army men and a dad and his little boy, who I guess will sleep with his dad. These men are very nice and though the thought of sharing a sleeping space with four males seems weird, I feel safe.

Bai Qiu En: Dr. Norman Bethune

I showed them a picture of my kids and said what Haiwu taught me, "*Wo shi Jianadaren*" ("I'm a Canadian"). Considering how so many other Chinese have reacted to my nationality, I should not have been surprised. The men looked at me, put their hands together, bowed and said, "*Bai Qiu En*" (something like bye-chee'yo-enn)—Bethune. Oh my! By association, I am being categorized with a man Chinese people honour and esteem highly. I feel extraordinarily humbled.

Heaven

Since departing this morning, I've reread and titled all the entries in this journal, the first beginning in mid-January when I had no idea where in the world (that is, in China) I'd go for my month's holiday. The most prevalent comment I notice is about happiness. I have so much love in my heart for Chinese people. Though this journal is far from full, I've been bold enough to write a title on its cover "Heaven."

I am grateful for this opportunity to travel. Not many years ago as a foreigner I'd have been barred entry to this country. Later, I'd have been allowed in but denied the freedom to travel, be on my own or to take photos. Most Chinese people would have been forbidden to speak to me. Now here I am travelling freely on my own, talking to anybody I want and taking pictures. I feel more confident of my personal safety than I would in a lot of other places.

Think for Yourself

While travelling on that train, I reflected on my growing empathy with Chinese people. For all that I was learning, I was grateful. I observed and asked questions. My young friends helped me to understand many things. I remembered a thought-provoking conversation I'd had with Yeming over a month before.

"Ramona, what differences do you notice between Chinese and Canadians?"

"Canadians are freer in sharing their opinions."

"Can you give me an example?"

"I'll tell you in terms of teaching. In my Canadian classes we discuss lots of different issues. I encourage critical and creative thinking."

Yeming was already familiar with these terms. I'd spoken about them in our HIT conversation class. "You don't find much here, right?" he said.

"Not much. I told my HUST students that classroom rule #1 is 'Think for yourself.' They found that hard at first."

"It hasn't been encouraged here. Do you understand why?"

"Because the system is entirely different. With a huge population, it's easier to keep control if people don't question things or think too much for themselves. Right?"

"Maintaining law and order is important." Yeming was matter-of-fact.

"Yes, but..."

"We have an idiom which might help you understand: '*qiang da chu tou niao*.' It means the bird that puts its head out of the nest will have its head shot off."

"Not too subtle, is it? Physical and social survival?"

"Yes."

"Best not to draw attention to yourself, lie low, don't stand out?"

"Yes. That is changing."

"I hope so. Actually, I believe you. People still need to be cautious. With 9/11 and what happened afterwards, I feel more cautious than before."

"Ramona, we have another idiom that's similar. It has a positive meaning. '*Tao guang yang hui*.' It means to 'hide your light and nourish your weaknesses.'"

"The part about 'hiding your light' must be about staying humble."

"Yes. Modesty is important. Chinese people traditionally do not like to show off. We don't like to offend others. A low-key manner is good."

"I like that. Maybe that's one of the reasons I am comfortable in China. What about 'nourishing your weaknesses?'"

"It means to strengthen the things you are not good at. Deng Xiao Ping reminded Chinese people about this ancient idiom. In our culture it's important to be realistic. We need to know about our abilities and our disabilities. We need to work hard to improve."

"My HUST students talk a lot about needing to work hard and about improving. This is my experience of China. Hard-working people, almost everywhere I look."

"Yes, we work hard. We want to improve ourselves and China too."

"This too is generally my experience of Chinese people. It's amazing—all that in four characters!"

"Do you understand how *tao guang yang hui* is different from the bird idiom?"

"You don't get killed if you happen to stand out?"

"Yes. This one says that when the time is right, it's good to express yourself. Doing so suddenly is okay. You won't be hurt. People will be surprised in a good way."

"I like this one, Yeming. I don't like showing off. I also like to improve myself."

"I think Chinese people can feel this, Ramona. Maybe that is why we feel comfortable with you."

"Oh thank you."

"You also like to learn about us and we like that."

"I'm glad."

Saturday, February 5, 2005, 6:30 p.m.

Eleven More Hours

It's dark. I wish I could find one of those Gravol-type tabs. I'd take part of one later to help me sleep. I want to be up by 5:10 a.m. Yeming has travelled to Jingdezhen today and will spend the night there so he can meet me at 5:30 a.m. Leaving a prosperous province and going to a poor one, I wonder what I will see.

We've just arrived in Nan Ping Bei Zhan (Nanping North Station). I'm glad there's an English sign. In my English atlas, this city looks like a largish place, so I imagine we'll be sitting here for a while. We appear to be halfway to Jingdezhen.

I've been reading a collection of Chinese short stories Haiwu lent me, borrowed from the HUST library—one page Chinese and the facing page English. *A Madman's Diary and Other Stories*, a classic by Lu Xun. He was a brilliant writer of satire, Haiwu told me. In middle school Haiwu had to memorize and recite passages from some of Lu Xun's essays and stories.

Arrival in Jiangxi Province

Sunday, February 6, 2005, 10 p.m. Jingdezhen, Jiangxi Province

Tired and Happy

My brain feels fried with intense fatigue. We're now at Yeming's relatives' home.

On the train, which already seems a week ago, I barely slept—maybe two to three hours. Yeming met me and we came here to his aunt and uncle's in Jingdezhen. When we arrived, I had a shower and lay down for a couple of hours, which helped.

Yeming lived here with his father's sister and her family for a good portion of his childhood. I've met his aunt, uncle and two of the three daughters and their husbands. One of the husbands is a train conductor—a sensitive, kind-looking man. With their smiles, Yeming's relatives have all helped me to feel comfortable. I like these people.

Yeming's aunt, uncle and other
family members in Jingdezhen, Jiangxi Province

Chinese China

Jingdezhen is famous as the china capital of China, where the finest of porcelain is made. It is exquisite, delicate and super strong. There must be a fabulous export business. This afternoon, one of Yeming's cousins, her husband and daughter took us out. We saw an artisan at work, sculpting a 2½-3 foot tall figure of Shou Xing, the Taoist god of longevity. His name means "the star of human life." The things I learn!

I bought a couple of lidded tea cups to give as gifts to Liyi and Songhe when I return to Harbin. Already I have carefully wrapped them up in clothes and put them in the middle of my bag. I love the lamp standards in the downtown streets. They are all porcelain and so pretty!

As we made our way back to the aunt and uncle's, I saw something strange and disturbing. I wasn't at all sure what the man was carrying upside down, with its back resting in his hands and its legs sticking straight up in the air. It looked like an animal stiff with rigor mortis. A dog? I asked Yeming, who quickened his step and said, "Don't look. Just forget it." It's the only time I've seen anything like this in China.

It's Raining, It's Pouring ... la la

After supper, as if I weren't tired enough, I agreed to go walking with Yeming to a recreation centre. It was raining and I started singing the children's nursery rhyme "It's Raining, It's Pouring." The next thing you know, Yeming and I were singing it together and jumping over puddles, all the way to the rec centre. I had a blast playing table tennis, a very popular and competitive sport in China.

In the morning, we leave to get the train to a town called Wannian near Yeming's hometown. Soon I will meet his immediate family.

Monday, February 7, 2005, 7:42 p.m. (Drab, cold weather) Across the river from Zibu

Day of Wonder, Filth and Beauty

An utterly amazing day. I arrived at my destination. The town of Zibu is pronounced like zip with the p dropped, then boo! I'm across the river from the town, on the second floor of the family's three-story house in a kind of big middle room between two big bedrooms. This is the "old home." From Yeming's computer and excellent speakers, I'm thoroughly enjoying Chinese popular, easy-listening music and for the first time all day, I am getting warm. An electric heater has been turned on solely for my benefit.

Yeming put into my hands a copy of the book he's reading, Dickens' *Tale of Two Cities* in English. It's a superb book, a challenging read, and Yeming is obviously understanding it. The smarts of my young Chinese friends impress me.

Absurdly Awful

This has been a day of wonder, filth and beauty, a day that has been so awful in some ways that it's absurd and I can't stop myself from laughing out loud! First there was the train ride to Wannian from Yeming's aunt's and uncle's in Jingdezhen. Yeming and I were talking about English idioms and how one little preposition can make such a big difference (e.g., "to put up, to put up with, to put on, to put upon, put out, put off, put through, etc.). Sitting on a train chatting about linguistic matters, I swear we could have been super stars in a top-rated movie for the rapt attention we got.

I mostly try to ignore staring but every now and then I look at gawkers, smile and say, *"Ni hao."* Some smile back, some look away embarrassed and others just keep staring without so much as a blink of an eye. The staring, which I usually tolerate, was hard to take.

We arrived in Wannian, perhaps the dirtiest town I have ever been in, in terms of garbage and mud. Making our way through the traffic was positively unnerving due to driver craziness that was worse, I swear, than that of Harbin. Our bus to Zibu turned out to be a van. It was almost full, but since I'm a "VIP" I was given the front seat. I was glad of a seatbelt. We drove for about half an hour through sparsely populated, barren, red-soil countryside, winter bleak with masses of mud everywhere. The road, however, was paved and in good condition. The driver had music blasting. It was some fast-paced, techno-crappo, bass-dominated version of the normally great Russian song "Kalinka." It was head-achingly loud.

Not Even One Grain of Rice

While Yeming and I travelled that day, he drew my attention to the meagre trees, which grew on wasted hills and flat expanses.

"There used to be huge forests growing here. Do you know what happened?"

"Haven't a clue."

"When Mao wanted to be strong like the West, he ordered all the trees cut down. He needed fuel for the country's steel production. Farmers had to leave their fields to manufacture steel. Nobody knows how many people starved to death. Maybe over one million."

"Really! This helps me understand some things better. Remember in that restaurant in Harbin? You picked up the last grain of rice and told me, 'Farmers work very hard to bring us food. We mustn't waste it.'"

"Yes. There is a famous poem about that. At one time my family was very poor."

"Yeming, I've read lots about how Mao did really good things for China at the beginning, then really bad things later. My friend Liyi told me what Chinese people now say, '70-30, meaning 70% good and 30% bad.'"

"We have an expression. *Da jiang shan rong yi, zuo jiang shan nan.* To conquer a country is easy. To govern it well is hard."

Monday, February 7, 2005, 8:20 p.m.

What Beauty?

I referred to this day as being one of wonder, filth and beauty. What beauty? Plainly and simply, my relationship with Yeming. He's a wonderful friend. I know he's wanted me to visit his family. At the same time, I've perceived an underlying reluctance. I think I'm starting to understand now.

The New Home in the Town of Zibu

Older ways are practised here. This is Old World China, undeveloped China, countryside China. Now Zibu, what can I say about this mud-hole of a town? My first impression besides the muck is of garbage and gawkers. Yeming says he's always stared at because he's tall, at least six feet, and because his father is the richest man in town.

When we arrived in the town of Zibu early this afternoon, Yeming and I made our way through grungy slop until we came to the family's new home. Even though Yeming had already told me about it, I was still surprised. The tallest building around, its gleaming white five-floored construction is an anomaly. The old home across the river, where they still live and where we are now, is far more classic. It looks distinctly Chinese, not like the new place.

Anyway, back to the stark white new home in Zibu proper. First, I met Yeming's newlywed sister and her husband. They were very pleasant. Smiling and other body language are pretty much the only way I can communicate with anyone except Yeming. Despite the dampish cold, maybe 1 degree C, Yeming's sister was outside washing what looked to be some outerwear on a scrub board with both a kettle and a hose beside her. I'm glad she was dressed warmly and wearing rubber gloves.

Then I met Yeming's father, a handsome well-groomed 49-year-old businessman who started the construction of this, their "new home," a year ago. There's one more year, apparently, until it's completely finished inside.

Yeming and I went inside, climbed up to the third floor,

then walked along an outside corridor. I left my stuff in a room with a made-up double bed and no key. We used a hotel or motel kind of pass card. There were many rooms like this that mystified me. Yeming showed me around the place, including the fifth-floor dance room with bar, strobe lights, sound system, sound room and TV for karaoke. Yeming made my day by putting on "*Lao Shu Ai Da Mi.*"

The dancing penthouse, as fine as it is, overlooks mud, garbage, brown backwater, and other buildings that are markedly less grand. The ground level floor is in the early stages of being outfitted as a spa with sauna and steam room. It'll be "for men only."

Although I've been told this new home is not a motel, it seems opulent amid some squalor. Maybe it will be their new home with extra rooms to let? Weird. Could there be big plans to develop this town? What does Zibu have to offer?

Yeming and I wanted some lunch and could find no eating place open due to the upcoming Spring Festival. We visited his older sister Yanhong, a beautician, in her business. She left her customer for a couple of minutes to find us a place, a filthy little dive (they may all be), where I ate the tastiest food this whole trip. A local dish with tofu, some little meat slices, shreds of Chinese cabbage, onions, and a savoury sauce. I'd like to know how to make it.

In the late afternoon we walked with Yeming's dad through even more mud created by a heavy squall to the barge-like ferry that would take us across the river to their family's long-time home. The ferry's motor cut out a few times which I did not like. If there were oars, I could not see them. No one seemed concerned, so I pretended not to be concerned either.

The Old Home Across the River from Zibu

We made our slippery way to the family's distinguished old three-story home and, like every other place, freezing cold. I swear, by late afternoon, the temperature must have been near zero (no ice) and -10 with the wind chill factor. I have been colder here than I have in frigid Harbin with its "mega" minus temperatures because Harbin has a dry cold and buildings are heated. Here the cold is wet, buildings are not heated and people leave doors and windows open. They don't seem to bother shutting the damp out, maybe because the outside is warmer than their unheated interior refrigerators. I don't imagine they particularly like cold but that's how life is.

Yeming's old home where I stayed, across the river from Zibu proper. Painted on the concrete wall, a government slogan, promoting the country's one-child policy, aims to influence the traditional idea that only a son can carry on the family name. It says "Giving birth to a son is the same as to a girl; a daughter is also your descendant."

The government in Beijing determines the central heating policy of the country. Coal is the fuel and I imagine austerity's the name of the game. There's a geographical divide: north of a certain mountain range and river, central heating gets turned on at a set time. Maybe the date varies depending on how far north you go. In Harbin, I seem to recall it was late October.

South of the divide, there's *no* heat. Never mind if it's cold south of the line.

Near the family's old home, girls in their bright new Spring Festival clothes. The town of Zibu is across the river, which we crossed by means of a ferry, much like a motorized raft. The family's new 5-story home is the tallest building.

'This is the Countryside'

Something I cannot believe about this old home is that there is no toilet. When I asked, I was taken outside into a little courtyard and shown into a cubby hole of a room with a low ceiling. When I pulled the string hanging from the ceiling to turn the bare light bulb on, I saw the plastic pail. Well, I peed in the pail and I dread needing to do anything more than that. When I tried to get an answer from Yeming about why this place doesn't have a toilet, I found his responses rather lame. Finally he said, "This is the countryside." It was like "enough said, thank you very much!"

In my mind, I compared the squat toilets in the Fujian mountain hovels. Mind you, they were by the pigs but still, they were toilets. I asked, "Where is the waste dumped?" Poor Yeming. Maybe I was being kind of thick. It's not that I wanted to put him on the spot, it's just that I'd never experienced anything like this before. He didn't "understand" my question and after I reworded it a couple of times with no success, I burst out laughing at the absurdity.

Monday, February 7, 2005, 10:45 p.m.

Warmth

I'm in a large room solo in a double bed with a heating pad. Thank God I don't have to freeze tonight! Yeming's mom is very thoughtful. They might not be as outgoing as Haiwu's family, but they are still good-hearted people and it's obvious they want me to be comfortable. It's a difference in temperament, that's all.

Up against one wall, almost to the ceiling, are stacked brand new comforters and pillows still in their packaging. Are these for the new home that's like a motel but isn't a motel? I wonder what that is all about. I have a pail in this room. I dreaded the thought of making my way in the dark down the stairs through the courtyard to the little room with its plastic pail.

A Remote, Across the River Place

Before I turn off the light, I have one more reflection on this day of "wonder, filth and beauty." Many hours ago, Yeming and I left the city of Jingdezhen, which was large, bustling and attractive, to travel to places progressively smaller, quieter and less attractive. I was happy to leave Wannian, even if it meant driving through miles of devastated countryside to get closer to our destination. From the small town of Zibu, remote in its own right, we then crossed a river to Yeming's childhood home in a yet more remote place. If I consider how we've journeyed from a big, noisy outer kind of world to a small, peaceful inner kind of world, then this day has been remarkable. I feel privileged to be here now. Perhaps I'm the only foreigner, or one of very few, who has ever been to this remote, across-the-river place. In future, I may well look back at this experience with puzzlement and awe.

The Answer

It took a while but I finally got my answer about the plastic pails and the disposal of waste.

"Yeming, tell me this time, please. What's done with the contents?"

"Don't worry. My mother will look after it."

"What does she do with it?"

"Don't worry."

"You must tell me."

"Okay. She dumps it in the river."

They'd installed toilets in their new home, yet even they flushed straight into the river. I found the situation disturbing. The first time I saw fishermen with their day's catch, I decided I'd better be careful not to eat any fish. It made me wonder if untreated sewage was ever dumped into waterways in Canada. I doubted lakes and rivers but what did I know? What about the sea?

Tuesday, February 8, 2005, 11:05 a.m.

"Dance Me to the End of Love"

Yeming is busy downstairs but I must say he's full of surprises. Music from his computer got me up and out of bed this morning. It was Leonard Cohen himself singing! It was delightful and amazing that Yeming had downloaded this song onto his hard drive. Oh, how I want to learn to waltz.

I hold a memory of Harbin dear in my heart. One night in the fall I stayed late at work. The building was silent, until I noticed the hauntingly beautiful music. It was not Chinese and not quite like anything I'd heard before. I wondered where it was coming from and who the male singer was, singing in a language I didn't recognize. When I looked down the seven floors of the atrium, I could hardly believe my eyes. On the first level, from one end to the other, students were ballroom dancing. I made my way down and hid behind a pillar to watch.

The unexpected beauty of those students and the romantic quality of the melody touched a chord deep inside.

Sweet and Innocent Memory Lane

Yes, I have so many little memories and they are all special. Since I have plenty of time, I shall meander along this pathway, the kind that safeguards the most innocent and tender of them. When have I felt touched or moved in this land of over a billion?

How about that misty November morning in Harbin when I cut across the Heilongjiang University campus? It must have been shower day for the girls' dorms. I walked behind two girls, each carrying her little basket of toiletries on her outer arm, while linking her inner arm with the other girl's. *They epitomize China for me*, I thought. Innocence and delightfulness, like spring's first crocuses poking through January snow. Time and again, this has been my experience of young people especially. There's a complete lack of guile and no thought to be cool. This may change over time but for now it's precious.

The innocence applies not only to the young. I think of the security guard at the construction site of the new HUST library with his dark, leathery-looking skin. When the weather turned cold, he wore a long, double-breasted Russian-style army coat and one of those big, black, Russian fur hats with flaps to cover the ears. Every time I walked by, I tried to get him to look at me. It took a long time but he finally did. I gave him a big smile and said, "Ni hao." He gave me a million-dollar smile back, revealing his few teeth, and nodded at me. He made my day!

The man who sold me noodles at lunch time in one of the cafeterias on campus is another memory. I loved the way he beamed and tried to teach me Mandarin. I'd point to the noodles I wanted, then he'd come around to my side, point like I just had, and say, "*Zhe ge*" (like jay-gah, stress on the first syllable), meaning "these ones."

The janitor at our apartments had likely never had attention paid to him by a foreigner until I came along. I liked his shy yet friendly manner. He grinned from ear to ear when I had Charles ask him if he'd like an English name. By George, yes! George was indeed proud to be called George.

Last but not least is Charmaine, the loveliest photocopy lady I'd ever want to meet. She was happy to receive a Western name from me too. She proudly showed me pictures of her twin daughters. I tried telling her how I want to meet them one day.

And the list goes on.

Tuesday, February 8, 2005, 11:45 a.m.

Back to the Present

I could go on and on but it's time to leave Harbin and return to the countryside in Jiangxi Province. I've been sitting alone, freezing cold, for the last couple of hours. I'm in the big room between the two upstairs bedrooms on the second floor. Yeming has set his computer on a table for my use. His mom brought me a portable electric heater, thank goodness!

I have seven layers of clothes on including jacket vest and jacket. It didn't occur to me to bring my ultra-warm Harbin winter coat. It's easy for me to be an ice block these days and I'm blocked in other ways too. This bathroom business troubles me. I have difficulty while travelling as it is. I'm here till Thursday, I think. Oh my.

Yeming's mom doesn't push food on me, for which I am grateful. She's a pretty woman who seems very shy. I wonder if she or anyone else has ever put her first. Somehow I think her life has been and still is a lot of hard work. Her hands are red, swollen and very sore looking. Cold water and freezing weather doesn't help. Maybe she's like Haiwu's mom and has not had the opportunity to go to school. Even if we could, I wonder if Yeming's mom would feel comfortable talking with me, her son's teacher from a university.

I was lucky Yeming and I could spend an hour together this morning. It was lucky because he says that's pretty much it for today, that is, in terms of blocks of time. He comes in here and in no time one of his parents is yelling, "Yeming!"

Banished Upstairs

It's the eve of Spring Festival so they're busy putting up decorations and need his help. I offered to assist but was told, "No, it's okay." Maybe they think that since I'm a guest on holiday I should rest and let them take care of things. The intention is probably kind and I am tired but I'd really like to be a part of the action.

I told Yeming not to be concerned about me. Though it's not possible to get online, I'm happy enough listening to beautiful music on his computer. He has many old and new songs played with traditional instruments. "Bamboo Under the Moonlight" and "*Bu Liao Qing*" ("Love Without End") are exquisite. I want to learn Chinese songs. Besides listening to music, I can read *Mad Man's Diary and Other Stories*, and of course I can write. For these things, especially the writing, I am grateful.

Falsely True?

As regards writing, I awoke extra early this morning and lay in bed thinking about finally writing a story for publication. The editor of a local paper back home expressed interest. I've been in China only four months and I admit I know very little. Still, my experiential perceptions are my own. Falsely true? I may be wrong, but it's true I've thought and felt certain things.

Actually, I'm a baby for all that I "know" and, like a baby, nothing can stop me from wanting to learn more. I want to know and understand from inside the heart out—mine and other people's. When it comes to me and China, my bottom-line remains the same: I want to write for publication.

What can I now say about Yeming, one of my most wonderful teachers? I can say he and I always enjoy great conversations. I learn about music, poetry, language, customs and history. It's an organic learning.

Ancestral Respect

One example of what I have referred to as organic learning occurred when I asked Yeming about a picture and ended up learning about ancestor worship and cultural differences.

"Yeming, who's that man in the photo downstairs?"

"My grandfather, my father's father. I don't remember him. He died when I was two years old."

"It's the only photo on the wall."

"Yes, because my father honours him."

"Sounds as though he was a special man."

"Ramona, come here. See across the river where there are no buildings, just a monument?"

"Yes. Very fine looking."

"My father commissioned it to honour his father."

"It's very noticeable. Is this an aspect of ancestor worship?"

"Yes. My grandfather worked very hard all his life. My father has worked very hard too and has become successful. We must thank our ancestors because they have helped us."

"You mean for the example they set?"

"Yes, but more than that. They worked very hard so we could have a good life. My grandfather did not experience my father's level of success. The monument is one way my father can show his respect and thankfulness. It is also a little compensation for my grandfather's hard work."

"Really?"

"Worshipping our ancestors involves complex beliefs. It's not easy to explain."

"That's okay. I'm just interested in anything you can tell me."

"An old belief in China is that the spirit of a person who dies is sad. He must leave all his family members and friends behind and he wants to linger. We are sad too. We want him to feel happy and comfortable to move on to the afterlife."

"That's an interesting thought."

"Yes. In China, the family is the most important thing. Even when family members die, we believe they still care about us and try to help us. We try to help them too. We have many rituals for them to feel happy. When we do not ignore them, they can be happy. They will like to help us even more. We help each other. So the monument is also to help my grandfather feel happy."

"Is burning money for the ancestors a ritual too?"

"Yes."

"It's fake money though, right?"

"No, it's real money. Real 'heaven money.'"

"You mean, you go to a store and buy 'heaven money' with regular Chinese money?"

"Right."

"Oh."

"Our dead family members can buy things they need in the afterlife. We want them to be more comfortable. We burn paper gifts too and leave special food for them at their graves."

"That explains the food left in the Chinese cemetery at home. Maybe you haven't thought about it, Yeming, but there are a lot of fascinating layers in Chinese culture. Canada is such a baby country in comparison and it's boring in some ways. I could spend a lifetime here and still not know all of Chinese culture."

"Yes, it is very rich."

"In Canada, I think we tend to look more towards the future than the past. Many of us don't know much about our ancestors. We usually know which country some of them came from. We aren't so aware of the personal sacrifices they made, like moving to a brand new country and starting all over again."

"Here we know where our ancestors came from."

"Of course! That's one thing that makes Canada and some other Western countries very different from China. We have people from everywhere, which is not boring!"

"What do you see that is the same?"

"That parents here and in Canada want the best for their

children. Actually, I think this is true about parents everywhere. No matter how good their own lives are, parents want their kids' lives to be better."

"That is true in China, for sure."

"There is another difference I see. It's about how you treat old people with respect and appreciation. I hate to say it but that's generally not how it is in Canada. The elderly are not always valued. We could learn a lot from China."

"Ramona, you help me to see my own culture with new eyes."

"It's the same for me too."

Tuesday, February 8, 2005, 4:05 p.m.

Feeling Misunderstood and Hurt

I hope things will turn around. A few minutes ago I felt so hurt it was difficult for me not to reveal it. I've stayed in this room all day except for three brief times downstairs: first for breakfast/brunch, second for lunch, and the third time Yeming asked if I'd come downstairs when he needed to shut the electricity off to rewire a light decoration for the festival. A little later he quietly asked if I'd go back upstairs. He was sorry and said it was something to do with tradition. He told me he'd wanted me to accompany him earlier when he "made sacrifices to the ancestors" but his father forbade it. It's not personal, I know. The man doesn't even know me and I am a foreigner after all. There's much I simply do not understand. Still, I feel hurt.

I'm provided with a decent warm bed and a heater to read, write or listen to music by. It's very thoughtful and I am appreciative. The food is good, which is nice, but I don't care all that much about food, especially when I'm not entirely in control of when and how much I eat. It's much easier here, though, than at Haiwu's. Here I can get away with eating little even though it's not as little as I'd like. I don't intend to be rude in any way but maybe I am. Rudeness is a culturally based thing.

Section 8

Father and Son

Writing has helped me feel more composed. The downstairs is beautiful with all the red decorations. I asked Yeming if I could take photos later but he said he didn't know. He'd have to ask his father.

Some friction exists between Yeming and his dad, typical father/son stuff. I feel for Yeming. His father is enormously proud of his only son, and rightly so. Yeming is a brilliant young man, the only person in the whole town to attend university and probably the first is my guess. He also happens to be a master's student at one of China's most renowned universities, the Harbin Institute of Technology. HIT is somewhat equivalent to the USA's MIT.

As an only son, masses of parental expectation rest on Yeming's shoulders. He is his family's brightest hope for the future and even his name suggests this. *Ye* means gloriously bright as a blazing fire. *Ming* means bright, clear, intelligent. Ye + Ming indicates somebody expected to have a bright and successful future. Yeming does not want to disappoint.

Success

I recall a conversation Yeming and I had about success. He expressed what all my students say—that, essentially, working hard at one's studies, finding a good job and making lots of money all equal success. I told him that success in the West is viewed similarly. Many people including me add good health and happiness. I then told him that an indispensable aspect of success for me is doing what I can to help the world be better. "That way, when I'm on my death bed I can feel satisfied that my life had been worthwhile."

A couple of days later Yeming said, "I've been thinking about what you told me. With my money I also want to help poor children in the countryside go to school." I felt moved by this.

Appreciation and Loyalty

High on Yeming's list of priorities is helping his family. His earnestness, loyalty and sense of duty are unquestionable. I see

122

these qualities in Haiwu too and I detect no resentment from either young man. Each is an only son with two older sisters and each son talks about needing a good job to support his parents, especially given all the sacrifices they made for their son's higher education. One day will these sets of parents live with their sons and their wives in the old way, I wonder.

Do Yeming and Haiwu and others of their generation represent a bridge between old and new worlds? Are ancestor worship and other old ways taught to children as much as before? "Modernization" may not be as rapid in Zibu but it's coming.

Maybe the current "capitalist revolution" is not as disruptive as the Communist Revolution. Still there's tumultuous change all over the place. It's out with the old and in with the new. "Don't throw the baby out with the bath water!" I want to yell. "Make changes of course but please, China, remember *xi xin*! Your cultural roots grow long, wide and deep. Don't indiscriminately sever them. Western influence is not all wonderful. Don't be beguiled."

I've been grumbling but I'm darned lucky to experience Zibu at this time. There's no McDonald's, KFC or Starbucks, at least not yet. Fast food equals crap food. Cancer, heart disease, strokes, blah! Rice, tofu, vegetables and green tea are good.

My HUST students tell me lots. They're 18- and 19-year-olds, many one child per family children. Some of those who have siblings come from rural areas exempt from the policy or their parents were well-to-do enough to pay a fee in order to have another child. Some siblings are many years older and so were born before the policy came into effect. There may be other reasons I don't know about.

At any rate, there are problems brewing up the yin-yang. I do not envy the lot of Chinese leaders today. One boy lamented to me in my office one day. "Will I ever have a wife? Not enough girls." Then he semi-brightened up and told me the solution. "Import girls from the Philippines, Vietnam."

Tuesday, February 8, 2005, 5 p.m.

More on the New Home in Town

God, thanks for giving me the desire to write. My feelings of hurt about being banished upstairs have subsided as I consider how much I treasure time for writing and reflecting. Speaking of which, I've been reflecting on the family's huge new home, built in a small town in a poor province. I wonder who would be able to afford the spa and the dance hall, not to mention who'd stay in the rooms that look exactly like motel rooms, except Yeming insists the place isn't a motel. What about all those new comforters stacked up against the wall in my bedroom?

And who, for that matter, would want to come to such a grungy town for entertainment and relaxation? When I asked Yeming as diplomatically as I could he said, "Businessmen who might be too tired to go home."

The suspicion I was already feeling, spiked. I was sceptical, cynical even. My thought was, *Sleaziness in the works, like pretty girls doing the massaging, et cetera.* Then not wanting to believe this of my friend's family, I tried to reason. *Given how public the place is, it's got to be legit.* Still my suspicions lingered, so I asked Yeming more questions.

He helped me understand a few things and now my head's no longer in the gutter. Business in China is often conducted by ensuring that prospective clients and/or partners are catered to and have time to unwind. This includes wining, dining and, in this case, providing accommodation something like the golf game and clubhouse dinner and drinks scene in Canada and the U.S. Mr. Zhang himself is a businessman. He made his money by selling coal for cooking purposes to villages up and down the river. He saw an opportunity in this town. Maybe others will too?

Zibu may be a little, Old-World China town at present but likely not for long. Come to think of it, if it weren't for the mud, the garbage, the cold, the staring and the lack of a toilet, I'd not be nearly so reactive. That's a lot to be reactive to, though.

Tibetan Wine New Year's Eve

Dinner was special with Yeming's mom having worked overtime on many holiday dishes. It was just the four of us. Yeming must have told her I love Chinese mushrooms because we had those—scrumptious! I took the smallest piece of chicken I could find from another bowl and it was the chicken's head! I couldn't even pretend so I left it in my dish. I wonder if there was any symbolism with the many different dishes and the way they were served. Probably.

Mr. Zhang brought out a bottle of wine and Yeming said, "My father bought this for you. It's Tibetan wine." It was a special gift. Mr. Zhang looked pleased and gave me a boyish smile when I took a picture of them opening the bottle.

"Everyone is having some, right?"

"No, it's only for you. My parents don't drink wine. My father wants you to drink it." I noticed Mr. Zhang looking at me.

"Yeming, no way. I'm not drinking a whole bottle of wine by myself. If I have to drink it, then you're drinking half!"

Neither of us wanted any but drink it we did. It tasted like rusty-nail water. I felt a little buzz. Thank goodness it wasn't strong.

Wednesday, February 9, 2005, 4:35 p.m. At the old home

The Year of the Cock

I recall some of my students in Harbin telling me about the upcoming "Year of the Cock." "Yes," I said, "but in English it is better to say rooster." I then told them the slang meaning. They agreed that rooster would be better.

It's Chinese New Year's day and I am in the heart of the People's Republic of China! This morning Yeming and I, along with two of his cousins, got on the ferry and went to the new home's dance floor. I was not sure what the purpose was but maybe they were working on the sound system. In my day pack I still had some of the CDs I bought in Zhangzhou. We listened to some 2004-2005 Chinese hits. Goodie!

Chinese New Year feast.
Yeming and his father with the bottle of Tibetan wine.

I had a wonderful gift today. I was able to shower and wash my hair. Yeming's cousin, Jingming, who lives on this side of the river too, told Yeming I could use his (Jingming's) family's shower. Yeming brought along a hair dryer so I wouldn't have to freeze with wet hair. The house is more modern in that it has a bathroom with a Western-style toilet, hot running water and a shower. There's a two-element hot plate for cooking and one of those gigantic clear containers of drinking water. It looks as though they needn't boil their water.

If I Could Only Talk to People

I like Jingming. I noticed his gentleness with a mother dog and her newborn puppies, which lay on a bed of straw in a corner of the kitchen. In the house were seven other people: two little boys and two little girls, a woman who looked like Jingming's mom, another who was probably his grandma and an older man, likely his grandfather, but I didn't know. "Mom" had a beautiful, friendly smile. Smiling is warm and inviting but as a means of communication it's extremely limited.

Yeming is the only one I can talk to and I must rely on him. He's not the most naturally forthcoming person, especially when it comes to relationships and everyday human matters. Without such information, I feel adrift. Life happens around me and I miss out. At Jingming's, I found myself longing to sit down with his family and get to know them a little.

One of the little girls had horrible sores on her hands, like blotches of red swollen blisters. I've seen these sores on other people's hands in Zibu, including Yeming's mom but not as severe as this little girl's. Yeming later assured me she had no disease but "chilblains." I've come across that word in English before but never knew what they were and now I know. They are awful sores caused by cold, damp conditions. They heal when the weather gets warm.

Yeming and I walked back on gravelly, muddy paths along with a pig and a few ducks. I don't believe there are any cars on this side of the river. I took a number of photos. The weather was drab but the red banners decorating the outside of people's homes were cheery. Cute kids dressed in their colourful Spring Festival clothes played outside, the little girls with pretty bows in their hair.

Yeming taught me how to say Happy New Year in Mandarin—*Xin Nian Kuaile*. It's a different character from the heart *xin* so has a different meaning: New Year Happiness. I wonder if *nian*, the word for year, has anything to do with the name of the demon. Yeming coaxes me to say *Xin Nian Kuaile* to the relatives. When I do they beam all over and give me two thumbs up, like "Aren't you a clever girl!"

Excluded

His family are good people and have treated me well. I have felt their reserve and I have felt unknown. I don't like feeling like a stranger. I've shared meals with the family and I've watched them set off firecrackers but I've been excluded from a number of Spring Festival activities. Yeming tells me there have been many interesting things that I haven't seen. I can't say why and I'm reluctant to ask him because he seems uncomfortable with this situation. Maybe it's because I'm female or foreign or because I'm non-family. Or maybe it's because they want extra time alone with their son. Perhaps it is a combination of some or all of those reasons.

I'm resourceful and have read some Lu Xun stories. Thank goodness Haiwu had a good book I could borrow. I've also had time to write and I've slept satisfactorily but I haven't felt especially happy here.

A few days ago, before Haiwu and I parted company he said something like, "You'll have an even more wonderful time in Jiangxi Province."

I told him, "No, not more wonderful. If it's nearly as wonderful, then I'll be lucky." What can I say? That Yeming is my dear friend and I'm sorry he's busy. I can also say that I am immensely grateful to have met Haiwu and his family.

Chinese New Year Day, aka Spring Festival

Chinese New Year, I learned, was the most special holiday of the year for over a billion people! I watched Yeming and his father set off firecrackers, not fireworks. It was a very loud, extraordinarily smoky production, what with every other household doing the same. They had a big roll with hundreds of little sticks filled with explosives that looked sort of like a roll of machine gun bullets. The ground was too wet to lay the firecrackers down, so father and son unrolled them around the walkway built onto the top floor of the house. They then ignited the explosives and whammo—a chain reaction of fiercesomeness. Every ghost and demon from there to Beijing must have been scared off!

Why is the Chinese New Year holiday so special? It's like asking a Westerner why Christmas holidays are special. Actually, Chinese New Year seems to be even more special to the Chinese than Christmas is to us. In Canada, I know families who don't get together for Christmas for a variety of reasons. In China at the New Year that is most unlikely. Whatever it takes, people get themselves home. I read somewhere that it's the biggest movement of people within a short period of time on the planet. I believe it. No wonder getting a train ticket was such a big deal.

What I learned was that Chinese New Year, more correctly known as Spring Festival, starts with the new moon and ends with the full moon about two weeks later. It is based on the lunar calendar, so it occurs anywhere from late January to late February. This of course is before spring starts, so maybe it should be called "Spring on Its Way Festival." Once again I noticed the special attention paid to the moon in Chinese culture. I loved it.

Yeming told me Chinese New Year developed from legends thousands of years old. It involved something about a demon from the bottom of the sea named Nian who liked to come on land every New Year's Eve to devour farm animals and rip humans apart. It used to do this until a wise old beggar showed the people how to outsmart it. They learned that the colour red and explosions completely freaked the demon out. Hooray for all the red banners and smelly firecrackers!

In preparation for the New Year, Yeming explained, people

clean their houses to clear out old energy, especially the negative, and make way for new. Spring cleaning? They light red candles and put up lots of red decorations, both inside and outside, with sayings about good fortune. On exterior doors they hang pictures of "door gods," and they prepare their most special dishes. Parents or grandparents buy new clothes and gifts for the kids and give them candy and *hongbao*, decorated red envelopes with money inside.

Wednesday, February 9, 2005, 11:42 p.m.

Dancing

I had an immense amount of fun tonight! I can't remember the last time I danced so much. Even Mr. Zhang asked me to dance. Right after dinner, I was told the family was having a party at their new home and we needed to "leave in a few minutes." It was not much warning but that was okay, since I was included. There were lots of cousins—all men, about twenty-five of them, mostly in their 20s or early 30s but only three women—me, Yeming's sister Yanhong, and his mom who didn't dance or sing at all.

There was no food, nor were there beverages of any kind but there was lots of karaoke and dancing to techno music with strobe lights. I think I was a hit with everybody. Yeming's mom, who seemed too shy to look at me before, smiled at me several times. Perhaps she liked my lack of self-consciousness. I danced up a storm and literally let my hair fly. I didn't even have to think about being a good sport. One cousin kept handing me the mike, wanting me to make whooping sounds, so I did. The karaoke English songs were the usual I've come across in this country—some Beatles, lots of Carpenters and songs from *The Sound of Music*. If I hear "Yesterday Once More" or "Edelweiss" one more time I will throw up.

It's too bad there wasn't "Auld Lang Syne," considering how often I've heard it since coming to China. That song is played all year long. They call it "The Friendship Song." I've only heard an instrumental version but if there are Chinese lyrics, I'd like to know what they say. I sang the karaoke of "By the Rivers of Babylon." As I said, I had a lot of fun.

On the way to the ferry to return to the old home, I asked Yeming, "Don't your cousins have wives or girlfriends?" He told me yes. When I asked him why they hadn't come to the party, his answer baffled me. "It's our way." There is much I simply do not understand.

This time the ferry's motor cut out even more than before. I felt uneasy but no one else seemed fazed. Afterwards, Yeming asked, "Weren't you afraid?" He said it in a way that suggested he might have been uneasy too.

Yanhong is a lovely person. She's sleeping in this bed with me tonight. We have separate quilts and she's put her head at the other end and is already asleep. I guess her husband and son are in Yeming's room.

Yeming is standing behind his parents and four cousins. The young man with the tie is Haiming. The car accident broke his pelvis. The young man standing beside Mr. Zhang is Jingming. Both he and Mr. Zhang cared for me in the hospital. A roll of firecrackers sits on the table.

Yanghong and I. The photo of the
esteemed grandfather is on the wall behind us.

Tomorrow I depart on the next "leg" of my journey. I don't know how much time Heather will have off. I may be experiencing Shanghai alone during the day, an overwhelming thought. Then it'll be back to my work-too-much existence in Harbin.

At times like this, I wonder where my life's going. I have mixed feelings. I don't even know how long the trip to Shanghai is—10 hours or 20 hours? It's time to move on from here, I know. However, I notice an ache growing in my chest, pressing on my throat and prickling behind my eyes. Though I've railed about the countryside, I'm about to leave its peacefulness. Tonight I felt more welcomed by the family. I'm starting to be known a little and to be seen. I'm more than just a foreigner. Perhaps this is the real reason for the achy feeling.

Back in Canada

Ebb Tide Dream

"Ramona, please don't cry. Tell me anything. I will do it." Haiwu's hands reach out for me as the heavy ebb tide drags me back to Canada. "Haiwu, I don't want to leave. I will come back to China, I promise." Pain continues to tug, dragging my heart and mind back into my body, my poor broken body in Canada.

Half awake, I reached for the CDs I bought in China. Among them I found *The Wizard of Oz* movie. Thinking of the love Dorothy experienced with her friends reminded me of my friends far away and I cried even more. *These tears are good. I know they're good*, I told myself as I woke up more fully to record my Ebb Tide dream.

Friday, February 25, 2005, 12:32 p.m.

The Healing Grace

Not only do my tears wash my face but also they help wash my heavy heart. I am able to feel more present. I've been re-reading journal entries of my days in Zibu, my life captured with the stroke of a pen on paper. I remember the ache and the impending sense of loneliness before leaving Yeming's family. In a way I'd not envisioned, I got what I wanted—a Chinese family caring for me as though I was one of their own, like a "baby bird under its mommy's wing," for three days in Chinese hospitals.

Down But Not Done

I've been down but crying has helped buoy me up. Now I can see glimmers of possibility. John Keats knew how to capture the down so well. He wrote, "My heart aches and a drowsy numbness pains my sense as though of hemlock I had drunk." I understand and it shall be different for me. Pain and sadness may be my experience but I make this declaration:

Neither drugs nor anything else will numb my spirit. Beneath sadness and despair, I'm glad to say, I notice an eagerness stirring, a bubbling. Perhaps it's the beginnings of a zesty defiance of fate. Oh, I like that!

I hear God inside me saying, "All is not lost. Down maybe but not done. I'm with you for better or worse." Yes, I want to believe that. I also hear, "Remember an amazing human being, Ramona, a role model like none other. Remember Dr. Viktor Frankl."

A "Viktor Frankl" Vision

Here's what I know about Dr. Viktor Frankl. After suffering extreme prolonged trauma, he wrote *Man's Search for Meaning*, one of the most impactful books I've ever read. The futurist Joel Barker, in the video *The Power of Vision*, revealed even more explicitly how amazing Frankl was.

What was it about this man that left such a deep groove in me? It was his courage and his ability to see beneath and beyond horror. His humanity. Frankl survived Auschwitz. When he arrived there he formulated three goals, which helped to support him and others. First, to survive; second, to use his medical expertise to alleviate suffering as best he could; third, to learn what he could.

Frankl's vision was seeing himself standing on a stage delivering the keynote address to an international symposium of psychiatrists. His topic was "The Psychology of the Concentration Camp." And what blows me away was that he did it all.

My Goals and Vision

This is no Auschwitz I'm in, but I figure if Frankl could live for some future tense by creating life-changing goals and a vision, then why couldn't I? A *goal* suggests a new direction, and a *vision*, a new destination. Frankl's personal example has inspired me. I dare to ask myself, *What stage will I stand on?*

My Goals:

1.   I will be walking normally by September.

2. I will be studying Mandarin at a post-secondary institution this fall.

3. By New Year 2006, I will have returned to China.

My Vision:

I am happy, in excellent health and my legs are strong. I swim with ease. I dance. My partner is of course attractive, a man with whom I feel entirely safe to be myself. He takes me in his arms and we take command of the dance floor, with strength, grace and verve. Yes, *verve*! I have two homes, one here in Canada and another in China. I speak Mandarin and I know Chinese songs. I am surrounded by love from many individuals, most notably my Chinese friends. As much as they are a blessing to me, I am somehow a blessing to them and to China. Humbled and happy, this vision feeds my soul. Amen. First, I must learn to walk again.

These days, before rehab and eventual *baby steps*, there's passive physiotherapy. Other people need to move my knee and turn my ankle. A more urgent matter, however, is this extremely painful, bloated gut of mine, which reminds me of a nightmare from last night.

Box of China Poison Dream

Trapped inside me there is something like a box filled with all the pain and poison my poor gut has been tortured with. The poison seeps out into my entire body. It's a box of "China poison" and I am fighting to force it out of my system. Oh woe.

Friday, February, 25, 2005, 7 p.m.

Oh Woe Some More

I'm still shaking. Two rehab students dropped me but managed to grab me just before I hit the floor. The accident didn't kill me. The crude rescue didn't kill me. Chinese hospitals didn't kill me. The flights didn't kill me. Will the Richmond Hospital manage to do it directly or indirectly by giving me a heart attack?

I hear the voice of Eria. *"Why did you go back to Canada? Why?!*

They almost hurt you more. I'm angry. You should have stayed with us. "
Yes, I'm sure Eria would choose words like these if she were to see me dropped in a Canadian hospital. She'd express the outrage I haven't.

Saturday, February 26, 2005, 9:45 a.m.

You Never Can Tell

A new hospital cleaner just left. I was ready to throw something at her when she went out the door. She asked about "the hospital scene in China." I wish I hadn't told her anything. Talk about reactive.

"You must be mad as hell. I'd be!"

"I'm not mad. It's not like anybody was trying to hurt me."

"Come on."

"Really. I saw a man make a mistake and I saw him pay for it with his life. It's hard for me to be mad." She reached for her dust pan and I could see her eyes roll. I gritted my teeth and asked myself, *Has this woman got a problem?*

"Well, you never can tell what'll happen next in a place like that. China's dangerous. You're here now and you never have to go back."

"Actually, I plan to."

"Holy shit, are you a sucker for punishment or what? After your bad luck? You really wanna get yourself killed. And those hospitals—cockroach-infested I bet. Sounds like they could'a killed you." *I could hardly believe this conversation was really happening.*

"Let me tell you something. I could get killed right here in this fine clean Canadian hospital. Two girls just about dropped me on the floor yesterday you know."

She wasn't so quick on the draw this time and had to scramble. "Still… you shouldn't ever go back there."

"I guess I see things differently. I've got a little story to tell you. Will you listen?"

"All right." She crossed her arms.

"There was an old Chinese man whose horse ran away. All the neighbours said, 'What bad luck!' He only said, 'You never can tell.' Then the horse came back and brought along a big wild stallion. The old man's son trained the horse and everybody said, 'What good luck!' The old man said, 'You never can tell.' The son fell off the horse and broke his leg. 'What bad luck!' 'You never can tell.' Then the soldiers came and forced all the young men into battle. They left behind the old man's son with the broken leg. Everybody said, 'What good luck!' And the old man said..."

"You never can tell?" I couldn't tell if she was being sarcastic. It actually didn't sound like it.

"Yes. For all I know that car accident wasn't bad luck. Some things are blessings in disguise and some things are the opposite." Her expression was hard to read. I slowed my speech and said, "I figure it's not a good idea to be too sure about things. I try to keep an open mind." The cleaning lady tightened her lips and shrugged. I decided I'd said enough.

Saturday, February 26, 2005, 10:50 a.m.

Wash Your Heart: Internal House Cleaning

I've had enough time to cool off. That was one provocative conversation. How ironic it was with a *cleaning* lady, considering the picture that's coming to mind. Haiwu and I are standing in front of a big rock at the Buddhist temple in Xiamen. On the big rock is a two-character message: *xi xin*, wash your heart. It didn't say "disinfect your heart." (I bet that cleaning lady does a lot of disinfecting.) Neither did it say, "Harden your heart and become judgemental."

Since *xin* means both heart and mind, *xi xin* means to wash your mind too. Good idea. Negative thoughts and judgements have a way of popping up fast and trying to make themselves permanent fixtures. For example, *Why did you tell that woman anything about China? How could you be so stupid?* or *What's the matter with you anyway, cleaning lady?* These are thoughts that separate my head from my heart and my heart from others.

I need to say to myself, *Listen to xi xin's advice. Notice how judgemental you're being about that woman. Arrogant too.* Right. I don't know what she thought of anything I said and what she thought doesn't matter. Maybe the story got her thinking. Okay, wash my mind and look at the dirt flow down the drain. When I think clean thoughts, I feel better inside. I'm kinder to myself and others.

What I've found in life is that it takes willingness and courage to face one's own garbage, baggage, demons, whatever you want to call it, and deal with it. It's the dirt inside that makes you say and do the very things that you do not want to say or do. Yes, willingness and courage. After that, the strength comes from somewhere. I hate it when others spew their garbage on me. What if everybody faced and dealt with their own issues—especially people in a position of power over anybody, like parents or government leaders? The result would be amazing, a world nothing less than completely transformed.

Judgement

That conversation has got me thinking about my attitude towards Zibu and area. While there, I bounced between judgement and non-judgement, especially about sewage and rudeness. I'm an advantaged Canadian, I need to remind myself. I've got to be careful about sitting on a high horse. Still, I have my opinions.

With education, expectation and government support, sanitary conditions would improve radically in undeveloped areas like Zibu. They'd have to. Legislate toilets, put in proper sewer lines, put garbage cans on the street, show people how to use them, teach the three Rs—reduce, reuse, recycle. Create incentives. I'm proud of the Chinese people I know who donate money to support the poorer areas' hospitals, schools and sanitation.

With communication, which provides its own education, cross-cultural experiences of rudeness would decline noticeably. How could they not? What about my experience of being stared at? Maybe my rude is not Chinese rude. Somehow I think it is but I don't really know. For the most part, staring didn't bug me very much during my months in China but the gawking during the accident felt like an entirely different matter, like a violation of my humanity. Was I angry or deeply hurt or something else? I don't know what to call it. Generally, I tend to stuff down my reactions of anger or hurt. It's not healthy.

What behaviour of mine offends Chinese people? It would be a good idea to find out, if they'd tell me. The way to widen the common ground has got to be communication with the sensitive and tenacious intention to understand. To understand is to counteract narrow-mindedness. To understand is to prevent hostility. To understand is to prevent war.

Self-Empowerment

Another thought is that I've often played a victim role in my life. In the accident I may have been an innocent victim but I don't feel victimized. I may be weak but I am not powerless.

A line from William Blake plays over and over in my head, "The cut worm forgives the plough." I understand. A colossal impersonal force hurts an innocent little creature and it forgives the injury. Nobody wanted to hurt me. I didn't die. I've got my wits still. I'll get better. It's just something that happened.

A line from Shakespeare comes to mind too, about a character being "untimely ripped from his mother's womb." That's exactly how I felt in leaving China, untimely ripped from love and nurturing, untimely torn away because of a violent turn of events.

I empower myself by thinking in these kinds of ways. I also empower myself by asking, *What's the karma in all this?* The fact that I have no idea doesn't matter. Imagination is what matters. Whatever the karma is, I must be cleaning up a ton from this lifetime and a thousand past. That's a good thing and a great opportunity, as a matter of fact. I thank God I'm alive. My brain's intact. I have things to do and places to go. I have good support."

I have self-discipline too if I tell myself that. There's a quote about Lady Luck's being "a haughty goddess" who can't stand wasting her time on slackers. If I want her help, I need to be disciplined to prepare myself for what I want. It's necessary to generate positive energy because fear and discouragement have a way of sneaking back in. I mustn't let them rule. Writing helps and so does talking to my Essence—God.

Dear God...

"I feel daunted. I don't know if I've got what it takes, especially when my tummy hurts like this."

"Breathe, Ramona. I'm with you."

"Yes."

"Now is a time for you to be weak so you can be strong."

"Yes."

"Do you understand?"

"Taking it easy is important for my healing?"

"Yes."

"Giving in to the weakness means I'm readying myself for the rigours of rehab?"

"Yes."

"Oh God, sometimes I feel confident and brave. Then it vanishes and I'm a scared little kid. This is hard."

"I know. Stay connected with me. These conversations are good."

"I need patience and determination, I know."

"Yes, and self-compassion too, Ramona."

"I can drive myself hard."

"I know. Now's not the time for that kind of energy. Remember the blocked river. It builds up in volume and strength slowly and calmly."

"Yes, I'll remember. I need to know something, God. I've heard that 'fortune favours the bold.' Is that true?"

"More apt to say, 'Fortune favours those who work boldly with me to help themselves.'"

"I'm willing to work with you. What I need is a metaphor to help me make sense of my situation. I need faith to believe in a bigger picture."

"Okay, Ramona. You're in the middle of an alchemical process."

"You mean 'base metal into gold,' inside me?"

"Exactly."

"Lessons to learn and spiritual growth?"

"Yes. All that inflammation in your body is fire burning up the dross, your dross. Purification."

"Oh God. My whole body's an inferno."

"Don't fight it. Remember the phoenix."

"I heard Haiwu tell me the same thing."

"He's a wise young man. The phoenix chooses the flames for a reason."

"That's an interesting observation."

"Thought you'd like that."

"Phoenixes may choose flames but I don't. At least not from any ordinary level of consciousness, but if I tell myself I chose the flames, then I can handle them better. It's a psychological thing."

"Whatever works for you, Ramona. This way of thinking is good. It reflects your spirit."

"You tell me not to fight the fire. I don't have the strength and anyway, what choice do I have if I want to know what I'm made of?"

"None."

"Submit to my circumstances."

"Surrender."

"Surrender and stand up to my circumstances. If I don't, how can I possibly know who I am?"

"You can't. Remember, your number one job is to stay connected with me and *to listen*. Did you hear me?"

"Yes."

"Be kind to yourself."

"You know me through and through."

"Ramona, you have what it takes."

"I hope so."

"You can trust me. Your welfare is my concern."

"Thank you, God."

"Remember, 'All in good time. All in God time.'"

"Yes."

"And Ramona, just so you know—I need you."

Saturday, February 26, 2005, 1:30 p.m.

I Need You

God's telling me "I need you" moves me more deeply than anything else I can imagine. We need each other. Wow. Was I conversing with God or with my Higher Self? Is the Higher Self akin to God in me? The difference doesn't matter. What's going on inside is what matters and it's good. It's so good it's moving me to tears. I wonder if there is a bigger picture I'm operating within and if there really is a special role for me that involves China. Maybe I'm creating or co-creating it. Perhaps I'm being used, with my agreement, in a good way. Though I don't need to understand, I do need to be with this.

Changing base metal into gold is a powerful image. Some

people believe we choose and orchestrate everything that happens to us, especially the hard things, for our own spiritual growth. I wonder.

Thank You, China

That cleaning lady conversation has got me self-reflecting even more on matters related to my well-being. My first reflection, earlier, was about me and judgement and washing my heart to clean out inner pollution. Now, it's about me and painkillers, anger and bad luck.

Painkillers: In China my mind seemed to provide a buffer from the levels of pain that could have unhinged me. As of two days ago, I'm done with morphine. For several days previously I took little. The only pain relief I get now is from regular Tylenol, not as strong a painkiller but less of a pollutant.

Anger: I haven't experienced any and I doubt I will. Time will tell.

Bad luck: The accident was not bad luck nor was it something that happened *to* me.

Philosophy

The helpful thread connecting all four reflections—on judgement, painkillers, anger and bad luck—is Chinese philosophy, especially Taoism, which I've been exposed to through reading books, consulting the *I Ching* and living in China. The influence has been gradual, gentle and deep. I didn't realize how much until now. Chinese philosophy has helped to open my eyes, protect me from harm, keep me sane and give me hope. Three teachings in particular have influenced me deeply. One is to emulate water, such as a river, and go with the flow. *Wu wei* is a part of this one. Another is to keep an open mind. "You Never Can Tell," the story about the old man and the horse, provides an excellent example. The third is to "Wash Your Heart," *xi xin*. I am present to gratefulness. China may have almost killed me but China has enhanced my life and continues to do so in ways far beyond mere survival. China also taught me how to see more clearly with the heart.

Seeing with the Heart

My desire to be seen is shy yet unabashed. I admit it. In China I felt seen in an unprecedented way, much like others felt seen by me. Words were not the medium of communication. The eyes were; that is, the eyes of the heart. I and others silently said to each other: "Maybe I don't know you much on the outside, but I recognize you on the inside, your essence, your soul. As I see your heart to be good and beautiful, I see my very own self." I experienced a beautiful and uncanny awareness of the other's presence flowing into and warming my own, as they felt mine flowing into theirs. It was a simple experience, and sumptuously divine.

Sunday, February 27, 2005, 7:20 a.m.

Wash Your Heart Dream

"I need my heart. Stop hurting my heart," I tell the young bride. She looks up at me and smiles shyly. It is Yeming's sister, the one who just got married. I don't know her name. She's squatting down in the cold rain beside a wash board scrubbing something. Whatever it is, the rain provides the rinse. I look more closely. It's my heart she's scrubbing!

I awoke hearing a line of poetry in my head that I wrote many years ago, when my marriage was dissolving: *"Kneading my heart, grief imparts a softness I cannot bear."* My face is wet with tears now. I'm the one dissolving.

It's a wash your heart dream, *xi xin*. My soul, I say thank you. Now I shall close my eyes again, rest my hands on my excruciatingly distended tummy and visualize something for my healing.

Fire and Water Visualization

A star in the night sky sends forth a highly charged beam of golden energy towards me. I draw the energy in with my breath, through the top of my head into my heart. With each inhalation, my heart expands and the fire already there glows more and more brightly. Soon, the fire merges with all the other fire in my body, burning, burning, burning, every flaw, every fear, every bit of hurt and misalignment. As if outside myself, I

146

see myself, a figure completely illumined, engulfed in flames emanating from within and extending from my body. I slow my breathing and the flames subside, leaving behind an ashy residue. I am intact and quiet. I cry, my tears turning into cool, life-giving rain which rinses away the ash, completing the cleansing process the fire started. Then I rest.

Sunday, February 27, 2005, 10:42 a.m.

OH Failure

Yesterday afternoon Scott, Valerie and Linda made a special trip from Vancouver Island to visit me. I felt touched that they would do that. Linda brought her "OH" deck of cards that are great for self-reflection. I have found those cards fascinating in terms of helping me access inner understanding or guidance. I drew one for encouragement and got the word "Fail." Pictured was a hand mirror, truly a means of self-reflection. After talking about it, we figured the card is encouragement in a peculiar way. There is no failing. My body is somewhat broken but I'm not. The hand mirror says it's just how I look at myself. I feel daunted by the challenges ahead of me but I'll take it one day at a time and stay connected. *God, can you tell I'm listening?*

What is failure anyway? Plain not trying is what I'm coming to believe. In my HIT conversation class before Christmas, we talked about heroes. First I told them about Terry Fox. I showed them a map of Canada and a picture of Terry running with a right leg prosthesis. In the Nanchang hospital, I reminded Yeming of that. He said, "Oh no, don't think about that!" Terry did not succeed in the goal he set for himself yet no one would call him a failure.

Next we talked about Norman Bethune. Yes, he saved many lives but not nearly as many as he wanted. The great mobile blood transfusion doctor died at 49 years of age from a blood infection. Could anybody call him a failure?

Fire and Water, What Shall I Say?

"I need them both to heal me this day." Yes, in my healing visualization I used fire and water. Earlier I recorded my wash-your-heart dream. My heart has been hurting so much that it feels as though somebody's been scrubbing it on a washboard or kneading it like bread dough. A young woman in China is washing my heart. By extension, her country is washing my heart. This interpretation feels right. China, along with me, is responsible for my being crushed and broken. China, along with me, is responsible for my healing on levels beyond the physical. Another way of saying it: I met with serious injury in China and it's to China and its people that I find myself turning, in thoughts and dreams for comfort and strengthening. Perhaps a better me shall emerge from all this.

I keep coming back to "wash your heart," a beautiful metaphor for personal healing. If I'd not gone to China, I'd likely never have heard of it. I feel moved by the statement's simple and profound message. Truly it's a gentle commandment.

I love metaphors. A few special words used non-literally help to capture what a language cannot otherwise say. Metaphors poetically fill in some of the gaps in language. Wash your heart is a water metaphor. Alchemy is its fiery complement.

Hundreds of years ago, alchemists hoped to transform base metals such as iron and lead into gold by subjecting them to intense heat. Incinerate the impurities and you are left with gold. Metaphorically for us humans, base metal refers to the imperfections or unrefined elements in our own nature. Flames come from emotional pain, often soul-searing and the result of loss. The base metal into gold metaphor tells me, "Don't resist suffering, be purposeful, discover your own essential gold and be a better person."

The phoenix, too, incinerates. Haiwu's prompting me to "remember the phoenix" underscores the goodness of the burning. A heart scrub along with my insides being burned out with inflammation must be doubly good. Pain has a purpose after all.

Sunday, February 27, 2005, 1:15 p.m.

Too Awful

Thud! From contemplating heroes and healing, I give way to misery. I am feeling anything but heroic right now. Reclining in bed, I'm nauseous. I eat nothing and can barely drink water any more. My tummy is gigantic—stretched to the max, 10 months pregnant size—and hurts worse than all the rest of the pain in my body combined. When will I be well?

Financial considerations are also bothering me. Talking to Nurse Jon is helpful. He has a way about him that always manages to lighten some of my heaviness.

"Jon, long time no see."

"Right, since yesterday."

"Jon, do you think I'd be foolish not to see if there's at least some insurance money coming to me from China?"

"I don't know about 'foolish' but it wouldn't hurt to check it out."

"I talked to my sister's friend who was a lawyer in China. He told me I can sue the deceased driver's family. I can't do that! But what about the bus company?"

"Heavy."

"All of it. I have to let it go soon. Like I need this?"

"Last thing you need. You find out what you need to find out, so you're freer to let it go."

"Thanks Jon. Good to talk to you."

"Part of my job description."

"You're an awesome nurse!"

"Think so?"

"Very sweet too." That embarrassed him I could tell but he took it in his stride.

"Best compliment I've had all day, thanks."

Still Investigating

My sister Rebecca was a tremendous help. I don't know what I'd have done without her. Once again I dictated an e-mail to her on the phone to send to Yeming.

Dear Yeming,

Thank you for trying to find out information for me. In China must drivers have insurance? Here they must. Are insurance companies in China difficult to deal with? Here they are. I was told I can sue the family of the man who died. No way! Did you find out anything about the bus company?

I received a message from Jonathan. He said Mr. Sun (the man from HUST who came to Nanchang) has been very helpful. He learned that the police did not write an accident report at the time. My sister's friend who used to be a lawyer in China said I should have an accident report. The police said they are "still investigating." Do you believe that? I think it is "B.S." This means "bull shit." In other words, lies.

I wonder if they will blame everything on the man who died. That would be convenient. If that accident had happened in Canada, the bus driver might be found partly at fault too for not pulling over and for being on his wrong side of the road.

Maybe I should forget about all this but I would like information first. I really need to think about what to do. Thank you for helping me.

Your friend,

Ramona

Insult Added to Injury

The Onset

Before that Sunday was over, I had more reason to cry. The severe constipation, bloat, and excruciating abdominal pains I'd been suffering gave way to uncontrollable diarrhoea. Just breathing caused me to be sick. Two or three nights before, I'd dreamed that a box full of Chinese poison was trapped in my gut. I wondered if I had brought home an Asian parasite. That Sunday night, a nightmare from my unconscious mind decided to join forces with the nightmare happening in my body.

Awful Dream

This is the countryside... There is no toilet... Don't look, it's terrible!... I don't know. I must ask my father... I'm sorry but you must go back upstairs, Ramona... The bus... NO!... Somebody please help me... I need someone to support my weight, please ask someone to support my weight...Then the woman is pulled out, her screaming's a sword slicing me in two... Stop, stop, stop!

I woke up with a blur of voices, my chest heaving. I thought I was lying on the ground again in the icy drizzle, with the people staring. I covered my eyes and started sobbing. Then I realized I wasn't lying on the ground in China. I was lying in a hospital bed in Canada and I'd been sick again. My watch read 1:10 a.m. Hadn't a nurse cleaned me up just 10 minutes before, and 10 minutes before that? I called for a nurse who came and cleaned me up. Then I called for divine help.

Dear God, I can't bear to sleep if I am tormented like this. My soul needs soothing, not scourging. I need good things, beautiful things to calm me. I drifted back to sleep.

Comforting Dream

We don't notice a difference. You are one of us. 'Wang nian zhi jiao' is a special kind of friendship, Ramona, the friendship of forgetting age difference. Do you understand my meaning?

Yes, oh yes, I do.

'Xiao' we say to other girls or to children but not to boys.

Chinese dragons are auspicious and magical, Ramona. My family thanks you for coming, my hometown thanks you for coming. What do you need? Please tell me anything, I will do it.

Haiwu, be my friend, that is enough. Eria, be my friend, that is enough. Yeming, be my friend, that is enough.

Exhaustion claimed me, then I heard nothing.

Monday, February 28, 2005, 12:30 p.m.

A.F.O.

This morning two rehab girls were figuring out what to do with me when Dr. Arthur whirled in. He undid bandages, ordered staples removed from my leg, and sent me for chest X-rays. I was also fitted with a fancy brace for my right leg, an ankle-foot orthosis, or A.F.O.

So now I am lying flat on my back, right leg extended, with foot pressed against pillows and forced upright, perpendicular to my leg. I'm now wearing an A.F.O. The bottom of my foot burns and my leg aches. Pain flames along the incision area too. Too much fire. All this and uncontrollable diarrhoea attacks too.

Monday, February 28, 2005, 5:10 p.m.

Afternoon at the Zoo

It's finally quiet now but what an afternoon. The Nanchang Hospital isn't the only zoo. Granted, there's no robbery or police here. A nurse runs in, sticks a bedpan under my butt then runs out. Through my open door, I see others running and lots of commotion. At ten-minute intervals I call for rescue. There's no response so I read my book, contorted on a bedpan. All the while, an old man calls out, "Help me! Please help me…" After 40 minutes, a nurse returns. "Sorry, it gets like this sometimes. The elderly patient? Oh, he's okay, really, just a little confused." As I said, it's quiet now. Thank goodness.

This Isn't Kansas

Where's a fairy godmother when a person needs one? Or how about Glinda, the good witch of the south? Or even the wizard himself, not that he exactly did Dorothy any good, but then you never can tell. She did wake up and find herself back home. I felt terrible so I decided to create some comic relief for myself.

Hmm… do I hear a man's voice?

"Ahem, hey Ramona!"

"Ah, yes?"

I'm sorry you're not feeling so good. You remember me, don't you?"

"How could I not? You're the Wizard of Oz himself! I'm pleased to have your company."

"My hot air balloon's parked out back. I might not get you back to Kansas, but how about a different place that'll have your spirits up and you smiling in no time? 100% money-back guarantee. You might laugh out loud too." *Winking at me, he grins. This is delightfully silly.*

"I'm smiling already."

"Okay then, step right here, right over here, as we open the door to Happy Memory Land. Ta da! Taking you all the way back to… uh… China? Ah, yes, er, uh… now, m'dear, you tell the story."

"Mmm, I like this. A happy memory and a real one!"

"Yes, yes, real memories are good."

"I'm going to tell you as though it's happening right now."

"Even better. I'm listening."

"Okay then, you sit yourself down and relax and I'll begin."

"It's January in Harbin, about a week till our big holiday. I'm heading to class when a young man catches up to me announcing: 'The inspectors are here! They are visiting classes. Can they visit yours?' *What inspectors?* 'Sure,' I say. There's a few minutes left of class time and the inspectors still haven't shown up. The same young man dashes in. 'Please will you wait a little longer? They will be here soon.'

My students are so good-natured. I can't help smiling just thinking about them! It's lunch time but they don't mind waiting. One boy takes it upon himself to sing a Chinese children's song about two tigers. 'Hey, there's a song like that in French. I'll sing it for you,' I tell them. *Frère Jacque, frère Jacque, dormez-vous?* When I finish the song, I add, 'And there's an English version too.' *Are you sleeping, are you sleeping, Brother John?* By the time I'm finished that one, we're really having fun, everybody smiling and laughing.

Then the inspectors walk in, accompanied by HUST officials. They are well-dressed, dignified men and women, 10 or 12 of them squishing into the room. Immediately they pick up on our vibes and start smiling. I explain, 'I taught them about comma use in English today.' I point to the blackboard with examples. 'While we were waiting for you, Ron sang a song for us. Ron, would you mind standing up and singing the song again?' Ron does a double take, pauses, clears his throat and stands up. *A couple of tigers, a couple of tigers, run so fast, run so fast.* All in Mandarin of course. (They told me the English words earlier.) The inspectors join the applause for Ron.

'And I sang them the French and English versions.' *Frère Jacque, frère Jacque, dormez-vous? Dormez-vous?... Are you sleeping, are you sleeping, Brother John?* I sing both songs all the way through. If the smiles were big before, they are even bigger now.

'Do you come from Canada?' one of the men asks me.

'Yes.'

'Will you stay here after first term or will you return to Canada?'

'I'm staying.'

He nods his head and smiles.

I can't resist and say, 'This is my best class.' The students beam, not expecting this compliment.

'Yes?' A different man wants to know.

'Uh huh, and they haven't even paid me to tell you.' I can't help myself!

A lady says, 'Is this really your best class?'

'All my classes are my best class!' This is fun. 'But really, these are good students. I like them a lot.'

As the officials leave I say to my students loudly, 'Okay, now you can pay me!'"

"Ha ha, Mr. Wizard, you were right. I'm smiling and laughing now. Thanks for visiting me." Winking and grinning at me again, he departs.

I lie in bed savouring the fruits of my imagining him and my recalling a real and oh so sweet memory from Harbin.

Tuesday, March 1, 2005, 10:45 a.m.

Care Through the Night

I am weary. Not that I like to record this for posterity but again all through the night I kept messing myself and had to be tended to fast or my poor bottom would corrode. The nicest person looked after me, a man from Beijing named Raymond. He'd get me all cleaned up, including ointment, then be back in no time to do it all over again. With every "sorry," he smiled and said, "Don't worry." He was a math teacher in China and now he's a student nurse in Canada. He emigrated to Canada four years ago with his biologist wife and 10-year-old daughter.

An Imperative

And, of course, we had our conversations. He told me an expression I'd never remember so asked him to write it down in *pinyin*. *Ku nan de ren sheng zhi hui shi yi zhi jian qiang de ren geng qiang da.* At first I thought he said it meant "A sharp knife makes a strong person stronger." Actually it means "A hard life will only make a strong-*spirited* person stronger." He emphasized, "No ifs, ands, buts or maybes." In other words, it's an imperative—it's impossible for that person to be defeated. I'll drink to that!

Baby Girl Dream

Before it disappears, here is a dream from last night, faint
now. *I walk by a crib with a large pink bath towel draped over it, just
like the towel I bought for myself in Harbin. I pull the towel back and
there's a little girl, somewhere between 10 and 20 months old. Can't
remember much now. It seems she was talking to me and I felt immense
love for her. The baby girl is a new me.*

Love Without End

A baby dream is encouraging and music that helps me cry
is healing in a different way. The Chinese titles and lyrics I do
not understand, except for what some people have told me.
For example, Meimei, a nurse here, told me one song is called
"*Bu Liao Qing,*" like boo lee'yow (rhymes with how) ching.
It's translated as "Love Without End." Teresa Teng sings so
beautifully that I drift into another world.

Whatever it Takes

Dr. Kendall, an orthopaedic surgeon and Dr. Arthur's colleague,
visited me. He helped me understand a few things.

"You want me to describe your right leg injury?"

"Ah, yeah."

"In short, a hideous mess."

"Yes?"

"A comminuted fracture. That's a bone crushed to pieces. In
your case the tibial plateau—lower part of the knee. Three severe
breaks with multiple fragments above." He drew a little diagram
to show me. "But we got you back together."

"A knee replacement?"

"No."

"A reconstructed knee?"

"You could say that."

"What about my knee cap?"

"Spared. You're lucky. Fibula was broken. Common peroneal
nerve was damaged."

"What can I expect from that?"

"You've already got drop foot. That's why you've got the A.F.O. We don't want you dragging your toes. You can expect all kinds of weird sensations and numbness in your right leg, especially ankle and foot."

"Nerve damage will just heal though, right?"

"Drop foot, we expect so. The rest? Don't hold your breath. It'll improve gradually, but exactly how much nobody knows."

"Oh."

"Your knee will never be normal again. Prime candidate for osteo-arthritis. Expect stiffness and pain. Rehab's a nasty one. Your gut problem's a definite set-back."

"Yes. I asked for tests. I want to know if I have an Asian parasite."

"No, the Chinese aren't responsible for that one. You've got a hospital virus—*clostridium difficile*. You'll hear it referred to as *c-diff*."

"Never heard of it."

"Antibiotics may prevent infection but they can cause major disruption in the colon. Fauna killed off. We're already giving you something to help get your gut back in balance. As I said, major set-back."

"How so?"

"Rehab's delayed. Scar tissue has more time to form. It's tough stuff and can impede flexibility in your knee joint. Not the best news. Rehab's going to be challenging enough as it is."

"But I am going to walk, right?"

"Do you want to?"

"Of course."

"Then you will."

"My will's the determining factor then?"

"Often is."

"My new mantra fits: 'Whatever it takes is what it takes and I've got what it takes.'"

"Good, all the power to you."

Perspective

"All the power to me," except I still managed to scare myself. I imagined how an infection might have necessitated the amputation of my leg. Dr. Kendall had not said that. Neither had anyone else. I knew I needed to shift my perspective. My self-talk went something like this: *If c-diff has been the price to pay for antibiotics that protected me from major infection, then I suppose c-diff isn't all bad. As long as I never get it again! The main thing is: I will heal and I will walk.*

I also considered the critical importance of my will—intention plus determination. I knew I had both.

Release

Being in the grip of c-diff awfulness was horrible but one good thing was apparent: the release of toxic waste from my system. Symbolically, I was undergoing a release of toxic thoughts and beliefs too. I'd written about *xi xin* and alchemy, symbols of washing and burning away impurities. The illness felt like both, a double whammy, not so much a cleanse as a purge. I was only part way through the ordeal, yet I already knew I'd changed.

News from Yeming

Yeming responded to my e-mail about insurance matters. I was glad he ended with two positive references. One I shall call "Forrest Gump encouragement," the other, a *chengyu* good wish.

Monday, February 28, 2005

Dear Ramona,

I am doubtful of the justice and the positivity of local government. I have no idea about the outcome. Maybe there is no outcome. The driver had no insurance. He operated what we call a "black taxi," which is illegal. As far as I know, the driver was kindred with the vehicle's owner. I asked

*my father why you don't sue the vehicle's owner. My father answered we
would pay a lot of money to the lawyer and the officers of government, if
we sue the man. It would take a long time too. And as a result, we would
have no compensation. So it will be a long and hard process if you want
to sue the man, but you can try. I will support you. We do not know the
identity of the bus driver.*

*Ramona, how is your leg? All of a sudden, I remember Forrest Gump's
running scene as his braces break away. You will be like Forrest Gump
and overcome difficulties. Do you like the movie Forrest Gump? Actually
this movie is one of my favorites. I especially like some sentences, such as
"Life is like a box of chocolates … you never know what you're gonna
get." People say, 'The world will never be the same once you've seen it
through the eyes of Forrest Gump.' That's the truth. Do you think so?*

*Cure for your knee takes a long time. So relax. Be patient. But saying is
easy, doing is difficult. I envy you for your courage and ability to cope with
the situation. You are my hero!*

*I tell you Xin Xiang Shi Cheng. This means the dreams in your heart
will be successful. This is my wish for you.*

Your friend,

Yeming

Mei Meng Cheng Zhen

I received more encouragement that evening from a lovely nurse
named Meimei, Little Sister. She said some things about fine porcelain that got me thinking. Am I resiliently fragile?

"Ramona, you are a strong person."

"I don't think so. Broken and weak."

"Only broken in your body. Your body will heal. I mean strong
in your spirit."

"Thanks. Sometimes I feel that's true and other times, I don't.

I'm fragile, physically and emotionally. When I think of fragile, I'm reminded of Jingdezhen. Have I told you I went there?"

"The very famous city in China? They make fine porcelain there. No, you didn't tell me."

"I'd like to share something. I only just thought of this. You know how porcelain is so fragile? Translucent even? When I was in Jingdezhen I bought two china tea cups with lids. I put them in the middle of my luggage. In the accident, that luggage got ripped to pieces. Guess what? Those cups remained completely intact. I was amazed. They didn't break but I did."

"The porcelain is like your spirit, Ramona. This is a painful time. I want to tell you two expressions we have in Chinese. *Shou de yun kai jian yue ming.* 'Wait for the clouds to open and you will see the moon shine.' This means 'Keep your faith alive in a difficult, dark situation and the light will appear.'"

"Oh, the moon will shine. That is beautiful. Thank you."

"The other is *mei meng cheng zhen.* If you are patient and work hard, a beautiful dream that is hard to come true will come true. You are strong, Ramona. Remember."

"Thank you."

Wednesday, March 2, 2005, 7:30 p.m.

Serendipitous Gift

Two nice things happened today. In the late morning, a young lady walked into my room and said, "Hi, I'm Melissa. I'm a music therapy student from Capilano College. I asked at the nursing station if there was anyone on this floor who might be interested in music therapy and everybody said, 'Ramona!' Might you be interested?" What a question! We had a good chat, my starting off with, "I work for Capilano College." I told her a bit about what had happened. She'll come back tomorrow with her guitar. I look forward to her return visits.

Dr. McFarlan's Visit

Late in the afternoon, Dr. McFarlan, bless his heart, stopped by again. He said he was sorry I got c-diff, clostridium difficile. We had a long talk with my doing most of the talking. A few times I almost cried and had to hold my breath to compose myself. He was quiet and waited. I'm not used to being really listened to by men.

"Besides the obvious, how are you feeling?"

"Not great. I'm not depressed but sometimes I figure it might be easier to simply not wake up."

"Oh?"

"Something I haven't told anybody here. I fell in love in China—*with* China. With the way I felt accepted by just about everybody…." I couldn't finish my sentence. "Being a foreigner didn't matter. People were good to me."

"They appreciated you."

"Yes, I think so. I wonder if I'll ever see my students again. I didn't get a chance to say goodbye. My teaching there, only four months, was the crowning glory for the joy I've always sought in teaching."

"Hmm…"

"You know about Dr. Norman Bethune? He's a hero there. Every Chinese person could tell you about him, yet hardly any Canadian could. He died in China, you know."

"Uh huh."

"I read something he wrote in a letter. It just about undid me. He said, 'It's true that I'm very tired, but I haven't been this happy in a long time, and I am needed.' Dr. McFarlan, I knew what he meant. I felt exactly the same."

"Special."

"Yeah."

"Would you go back?"

"I'm going to."

"Even given everything that happened?"

"Yes. The other day a cleaner told me I was crazy. She thinks going back means getting myself killed. 'China's dangerous. China's dirty.' Yes, there is danger. There is dirt.

But things aren't all perfect here either. A few days ago I was almost dropped on the floor by two students from the rehab department who were trying to get me into a wheelchair. And it's not an Asian parasite that's made me so sick. It's an infection from this hospital, this clean Western hospital. We're so antiseptic in Canada it can make a person sick. Maybe I can get myself killed here!"

"No! Uh, the c-diff is brutal, no question about that."

"I don't mean to be dissing Canada or anybody here. Things happen. It's just that people figure their perceptions are the truth. Everybody does. As Westerners we should stop wearing dark sunglasses when we look at China. People are just people everywhere, no matter what system they're stuck in, Communist or anything else. I haven't met one American who's happy to be identified with George Bush in the eyes of the world. Why don't we just understand each other or at least try to? As far as I'm concerned, we're not very different and we all want the same thing—good lives for ourselves and even better ones for our kids."

"Your feelings are pretty strong."

"Yeah. I can get revved. For all its awfulness, I've cried buckets for all the wonderfulness I've experienced in China. That place is not only *The Good Earth*, it's also 'The Good People.'"

"It was the people, then, who made your stay memorable?"

"Yes."

"Will you write a book?"

"It's an overwhelming thought but I have given it thought. Perhaps one day."

"No hurry. Ramona, you say you're not depressed and I believe you. It sounds to me like you're feeling discouraged. China may be your crowning glory so far, but it's not your last. You're young. You have so much passion. The world needs people like you. You're an inspiration."

Love Affair with a Nation

Falling in Love

When Dr. McFarlan left, I bawled. I considered how falling in love with China had been gradual, something that had snuck up on me. I remembered the exact time and place I finally clued in, though. Harbin - Christmas time - talking to Tom, an American colleague. He told me about marrying his Chinese girlfriend, becoming a dad, and not finding the time to go home for a visit.

"Oh yes," we agreed, our lives in North America were great in a manner of speaking but boring as all heck; that is, compared with our lives in China. The love-hate relationship with China? Yes, we had it, just like lots of other foreigners. And for us, like for many of them, love was the winner.

One of those other foreigners was a man named John Fraser whose book, *The Chinese, Portrait of a People*, I read while in the Richmond Hospital. Fraser was the Beijing Bureau Chief for the *Toronto Globe and Mail* from 1977-79. Foreigners were just being allowed back into China at that time. Fraser wrote about his "growing affection for the Chinese people" that turned into "an expansive love affair." After returning to Canada, Fraser wrote, "Like many foreigners who went to China and have known the Chinese, a part of me feels in permanent exile. It's an ache that just won't go away." I could identify. For me China was like the lover I had to leave.

Thursday, March 3, 2005, 8:30 a.m.

Dear God, I love the way you talk to me through dreams. If remembering them equates with listening to you, then know I'm listening. I had a delicious dream last night - a Chinese lover dream. I don't know what it means but I do know it's good.

Love and Marriage Dream

I'm showing two photographs of the same Chinese boy to a woman. In the first, he's maybe three years old. He's wearing a splendid outfit, like a little Chinese emperor. In the next photo he's bigger, maybe five or six years old and wearing an identical outfit. The child bears some resemblance to both Yeming and Haiwu. Suddenly he is grown up and standing beside me, tall and attractive. Again his outfit is extraordinary, reminiscent of the dragon robe of an emperor and/ or the elaborate garb of the legendary phoenix. Whatever it is, the young man is strikingly handsome. There's a powerful attraction between us. He leans over and kisses me twice on the lips. Then we get married.

I woke up all tingly, experiencing the excitement and vulnerability of youthful romance. With associations of emperor, dragon and phoenix, the marriage in my dream calls for a royal celebration.

This dream reminds me of fire and passion. A fire burns in me for China. Chinese emperor: fire, resplendence, grandeur, boldness. Phoenix: exactly the same associations. I'll burn myself up with passion (intense feeling), then rise from the ashes all restored to health and go back to China. I like that.

The young man in the dream resembles both Yeming and Haiwu. In my psyche, they represent a constellation of much of my China experience: stimulating, soul-satisfying cross-cultural learning and appreciation. They represent a "new China," the one I want to see, that is solidly and respectfully linked to its own rich culture but at the same time, a China open to healthy influences from other cultures. Like others representing this new land, neither Yeming nor Haiwu is a know-it-all. They want to learn all they can from the world but with no holus-bolus taking on of Western ways at the expense of their own cultural heritage, which they are pleased to share with others.

Marriage is indeed what this dream is about, a union of me and my passion. The marriage also represents a union of China and the Western world, a union well worth seeking. China's cultural richness stirs my senses. It's a treasure chest. This land intrigues me with its depths and I picture it in my mind's eye.

Treasure Chest

China is a magnificent chest filled with amazing treasures. Across its richly lacquered surface of mahogany, a dragon and a phoenix dance. It is the night of their wedding. Opening the lid, I'm taken aback by the softness of a warm moon-lit evening in South China. I breathe, from millennia past, the fragrance of jasmine and wild orchids. I grow mellow in the beauty of age-old melodies borne by bamboo flute, pipa and erhu. The deep chest overflows with all manner of loveliness and wealth. Strands of pearls and pounds of ancient coinage mix with ivory carved artefacts the size of hummingbirds' eggs. Brocaded silks - peacock blue, gold, sunrise red. Jade amulets and bracelets. Bronze rings intricately carved with minuscule fish, delicate flowers, forlorn geese and full moons paying homage to the four classic beauties of old. Complex calligraphy - poetry and song - I see as I unfurl scrolls made from history's earliest paper. Fine porcelain and "gentlemanly" bouquets of plum blossoms and chrysanthemums appear bright in all their glory. The list goes on and I smile, captivated by another land's rich romantic lore.

Music to Heal My Soul

Melissa, the music therapy student, returned with her guitar and a book of music with hundreds of songs. I was thankful to have a private room.

"Do you cry? It's good for trauma release."

"Yes. I need to cry more. When I do, it's like I can feel lots of stuff coming out - gravel, mud, metal shards, broken glass."

"Pretty graphic."

"Yeah. I saw a man die and I couldn't do anything...."

"I'm not in a hurry. Take the time you need."

"It's not so easy for me to cry if it's just for me. If I think about that man though..."

"Did you know him?"

"No. He was just a poor man trying to earn a living. The driver. Thinking about him I cry or imagining when people first heard what happened."

"You may find music therapy quite powerful then."

"I know it is. I've got a discman and a stack of CDs. Certain songs really do it. My 'Sob City Songs.'"

"Oh?"

"James Taylor. Lots, but especially when he sings 'You've Got a Friend.' You know, the Carole King song? Every time I hear it, I think of Jonathan, the incredible young man who brought me back to Canada."

"What else?"

"Lots of Chinese songs. One's called '*Ding Xiang Hua*.' It's about a young girl who's died. The title's her name - Lilac. Another is '*Laoshu Ai Da Mi*,' 'Mice Love Rice.' And then lots by the best singer of them all, Deng Lijun. Her English name was Teresa Teng. She was super famous in Asia. Died far too young."

"Never heard of her."

"In the West, we don't know much about Chinese music. At least that's how it seems to me. Asians know all our big stars. Teresa was from Taiwan and was banned in China. Her music got in anyhow. 'The Moon Represents My Heart' is *so* beautiful! 'Goodbye My Love' is too. When I hear it, I imagine myself saying goodbye to China."

"Meaningful songs."

"Yes."

"Maybe we'll come across more in this book. There are a lot to pick from but I'd like you to choose two that really stand out. You know, speak to you for whatever reason."

Songs of Goodness

I found at least half a dozen and narrowed them down to "What a Wonderful World" and "Somewhere Over the Rainbow." The medley didn't even cross my mind. Melissa played them and I couldn't sing even if I'd wanted to.

"What a Wonderful World," I noted, was a song celebrating goodness and love, the simple things of life, much like Teresa Teng's "Small Town Stories." Meimei had told me that people in China heard Teresa Teng's song after the Cultural Revolution. They were deeply touched because the song is about kindness, beauty and truth, the opposite of the Cultural Revolution's cruelty, ugliness and lies.

"Somewhere over the Rainbow" I could not separate from its movie, my childhood favourite. I associated both song and movie with China. Since re-watching *The Wizard of Oz* in Harbin and then travelling in Southern China, I understood more clearly why I came to associate a Hollywood classic and one of its songs with China. In a word, it was friendship. The love and loyalty Dorothy experienced with her friends reminded me of Yeming, Haiwu and Eria. The feelings were deep. The song, Melissa commented, says dreams are attainable; they can come true. "Wonderful World" also has rainbows. Rainbows are about promise.

Meimei had given me another Chinese expression, "*Feng yu guo hou shi cai hong.*" She said it meant "after wind and rain is a rainbow." In other words, all trials are temporary; after overcoming hardship, things will be much better. Indeed, in both my culture and hers, rainbows symbolize hope.

Before she left, Melissa gave me a homework assignment to write song lyrics.

Thursday, March 3, 2005, 4 p.m.

Rainbow Bridge

Since Melissa's visit, I have been contemplating rainbows. What amazing phenomena they are, both calming and inspiring.

Fire and water combine to form a rainbow. Scorching rays from the sun filter through cooling rains from the clouds to create the beautiful arc we see in the sky. A few mornings ago, I combined fire and water in my healing visualization. That was a powerful experience.

Closing my eyes, I envision a rainbow, its colourful brightness shimmering as it extends far across the Pacific Ocean. It's a rainbow bridge connecting Canada and China. In both countries, I have homes. Fully recovered, I dance with others on this bridge that connects the two lands. I dreamily reflect, *Happiness is mine. My Viktor Frankl-inspired vision is a reality.*

Opening my eyes, I return to present reality, its monotone drabness meeting my gaze as I look around. The homework assignment Melissa gave me lies on the bed stand. I am to write lyrics for a song, which has a chorus and at least three verses; the first verse, about the past; the second, about the present; the third, about the future. The assignment is due on Tuesday when Melissa returns. So far I've written the chorus and I question my ability to continue. To dredge up horror is almost more than I can bear. I must focus on the promise of my rainbow bridge.

Friday, March 4, 2005, 7:11 p.m.

Walking

I "walked" today. Well, sort of, but it was a first. I got my butt to the side of the bed. Two people from rehab directed me on how to grab a walker and move my feet in such a way as to get onto a commode. Difficult. Later they showed me how to get into a wheelchair. Previously I had to be lifted and put into it. My tasks today represent small but big accomplishments. Exhausting.

As debilitated as I've been, I can still say I notice my strength returning slowly. My upper body has benefitted a great deal from the trapeze-type bars above my bed.

Today Dr. Arthur said we need to look at a discharge date! (Suddenly I needed to pee.) He asked if I were going home. "Can't. I'll be going to my brother's." Dr. Arthur said we'd talk more on Monday.

Saturday, March 5, 2005, 9:30 p.m.

Starving

I do more pushing, hurting and exhausting myself. I'm starving. Breakfast was insufficient, lunch barely palatable (so I ate little), and supper was good but not nearly enough, though I specified "large." When I'm this hungry, it's hard for me to sleep. Gee, my problem in China was too much food and here I'm going to bed hungry. *Wo bao le*. No, I am not full! It's a weird contrast. Ke ai de, where are you when I need you?

Comeback Story

I wheeled myself to the patients' lounge this afternoon and watched a special about Martha Stewart who just spent the past five to six months in jail, "a significant experience." Larry King went on, "Everybody loves a comeback story." It's another influence on my mindset. I am in the early stages of a significant experience in my life. I will have been in this hospital for about a month before moving to Ray's. Rehab will be tough. I'll work extremely hard, take it one day at a time and try not to feel daunted. My comeback story's going to be good.

Super Nice Staff!

When I was in the lounge, a nurse came to give me a phone message. I was surprised. She said she heard the phone ringing in my room and so answered it. Just about everybody on staff here is friendly, kind and helpful. I also appreciate that nobody bothered to take that telephone away. For all, I am pretty lucky.

Lyrics

I wrote song lyrics. They're graphic and make me sick. They're also uneven and need more work. Theoretically the assignment's good and realistically it's horrible. I quit. The only thing good is that I switch from being miserable to happy.

The song refers to Yeming by his English name John. It has two choruses with distinctly different tones. The first is mournful and sounds heavy and dark. It needs a minor key. The second is happy and sounds light and bright. It needs a major key. The chorus repeats after each verse. Maybe there's an echo repeating "Dying to live, I'm dying to live." The words living and loving must be stressed on the second syllable. Anyway, for the record:

Section Eleven

"Dying to Live"
(Chorus)
The day was grey, the mood was blue,
Time to say goodbye
to John
and horrible Zibu

Wake up driver, can't you see
The bus headed straight for you and me?
Turn too late, the sickening crash
Propulsion, pain, in metal trapped,
I see you driver, poor taxi driver, move and d-i-e
Moans and cries rise higher, high,
The gawkers gawk,
Why can't they care?

(Chorus)

Freed from wreckage, finally
To lie on straw
In drizzly rain
The gawkers gawk and
I could d-i-e

(Chorus)

John, how are you,
In this living hell?
Gashed by metal, cut with glass
ripped and bleeding, bruised and bent,
Somehow we'll survive this terrible event

(Chorus)

In Canada now, I lie awake,
Pain in my leg and

174

my heart does ache,
God, I ask you, help me please
To mend, to heal, to be made whole,
Restored in body, mind and soul,
To dance and sing and walk and run,
Pain-free with love for everyone

(New Chorus)
The day is bright
My heart does sing,
Time to open my arms
To blessed living

Pain-free, serene, restored am I,
With legs of steel that take me far,
Lungs big and healthy,
Heart full-brimmed,
Thank you God for this joy,
this strength, this new loving

(New Chorus)

China's still stuck in my head, understandably. I need to distance myself mentally as I have physically. When I'm *there* I can't be fully *here*. Shock has me in its grip.

Monday, March 7, 2005, 1:10 p.m.

Visitors

Yesterday many people visited me, mostly extended family members I seldom see. It was wonderful, though exhausting. This morning Susan and Mumtaz from Capilano College visited and brought the translated version of my Nanchang Hospital bill. I have enjoyed working with these lovely ladies, plus many other people at Capilano and HUST. Both before and after the accident, I have felt their support.

Hospital Bill Translated

Mumtaz kindly saw to the translation of the hospital bill. To begin with, I often find invoices confusing. This one, even in English, is mind-boggling. The three-page document lists dozens of charges and repeats several charges two or three times, using different figures. Only some of the services billed to me make sense. Randomly, here are a few of the charges:

- Third-degree nursing (39 rmb),
- Phosphate injection (223.20 rmb),
- HIV plus coagulometer test (100 rmb),
- Disposal stool container (4.10 rmb); revenue's gotta come from somewhere, and
- Central air conditioning (12 rmb).

The 6 rmb (about $1) for "guest attending fee" must have been for the floor space. More charges included blood work, injections, pills (I only recall one laxative), an electrocardiogram (yeah?) with "twelve computers," plus lots of X-rays. Was my elbow X-rayed? Oh yeah, it was. A deposit of 3,000 rmb was pre-paid. Mr. Zhang must have seen to that.

The remaining balance on this invoice, which a nurse brought to us on the last night, appears to have been 1913.45 rmb. Mr. Zhang initially refused to let me pay that small amount. We compromised with my paying half. I realize now he paid the lion's share. The more I think about my friend's father, the more of a modest hero he is becoming in my eyes. He did not need to be so generous.

A Few Reasons I'm Grateful to be a Canadian

Looking at this Chinese hospital invoice reminds me of my citizenship. I see myself a citizen of the world *and* I am most grateful to be a Canadian. How come?

1. High standard of living! Don't take it for granted anymore.
2. With a small population, our ingenuity and resources are not taxed nearly as much as many other places. We've no reason to be cocky.
3. Proper emergency response. (I want to know who those

Chinese men were who got me out of the wreckage and to hospital.)

4. Corruption *less* of an issue. Being "first world," not nearly the same impetus exists. (Still plenty here.)
5. Hospitals and doctors are more trustworthy. Hospital management any better? Doctors any better? Accountability? Maybe not, but comparatively speaking, my trust level is much higher. No price tag on trust.
6. Our medical system. I don't have to liquidate all my assets.
7. English language. I can communicate with people in many countries. Oh happy day!
8. Fresh air I can breathe deeply. Smoking is not permitted indoors.
9. Drinkable water without boiling.
10. Flush toilets and sewage-treatment plants.
11. Car accidents are treated seriously. Fatalities investigated. Police reports are comprehensive. (Have never seen one but I think so.)
12. "Free" public education. (List goes on and on.)

Monday, March 7, 2005, 5:40 p.m.

Rush is On
Dr. Arthur said we might look at a discharge Friday this week. It depends on chest X-rays and other factors. Then the physios all said to me, "Wednesday" (that is, earlier). If it has to be this week, Friday's way better because I'd have more time in this *safe* environment to develop extra strength and confidence. My heart's pounding like crazy. The big world beckons.

Trauma 99
I had a very enjoyable visit with Rachelle this afternoon. I'm grateful to have sisters. Something happened that was a bit startling and reinforced the miracle of my still being alive. Oh my, what I'm finding out! Rachelle took me in the wheelchair

down to the main floor of the hospital. Twice we cruised by Emergency. Each time a different man came out to talk and they each commented on the terrible condition I'd been in upon arrival and expressed their amazement that I'd been allowed to fly. Oren is an admitting clerk in Emergency; the other, Noel, I don't know what.

Noel said, "If you'd arrived here from a local accident, we'd have assessed you a 'trauma 99' and sent you straight to VGH. Your leg wasn't the issue. It was the broken ribs and punctured lung lining."

That explains why Dr. Arthur pointed to my right leg and then to the right side of my chest and said, "It's not *that* we're worried about, it's this." Broken bones have a way of piercing things, like vital organs!

Noel continued, "We knew you were coming. We knew you'd survived a few days in China and a flight, so we were ready to check you out thoroughly and keep you here." He ended up by saying, "You must have a mighty powerful guardian angel." Oh, I must! *Thank you God for protecting me.* Now I must get myself back to the present. Breathe.

Tuesday, March 8, 2005, 7:45 p.m.

Baby Steps

This day I have been doing a lot of getting up and using the walker, travelling short distances. It takes everything out of me and now I'm hurting. It's good in that I'm starting to get some shape returning to flabby muscles and my gut girth is normalizing. Nurse Jon wheeled me in a special type of wheelchair to a shower. Positively heavenly hot water pouring over me sure beats sponge baths in bed.

On the Brink

Melissa came and we started working with my lyrics to figure out a melody. She is very talented. I didn't tell her how this song business is on the brink of being too much. I don't want to believe it myself. I want to be stronger. She'll be back tomorrow.

Wednesday, March 9, 2005, 8:50 a.m.

Gold Mine

Last night was a gold mine for dreams. Two stand out: a baby dream, my second in a week, and a weird one about an annoying woman. Writing them out may help me decipher them.

Baby Boy Dream

All of a sudden, I give birth to a big baby boy. It's like I didn't even know I was pregnant. He must be at least 10 pounds. His father is there, a man I do not know. I think, "Oh my, I must have had sex with this guy. Why would I have done it without ensuring some kind of contraception?" He reminds me of an American actor I saw momentarily in a sci-fi show on TV in the lounge the other day. I notice he smokes, which is a real turn-off. Somebody hands the baby to another woman who starts to breastfeed him. I say, "Hey, I can nurse him myself." I take the baby and start to nurse him. I don't think I particularly like this dad but it seems he's into "being a dad." Changing diapers and so on. Seems to me he's on the phone to another woman at some point.

Dream Exploration

It's such a puzzle. I thought that chatting with the main players might help. I've asked each, "What do you have to tell me? What should I know about you?"

The baby tells me: "You already know what I'm going to tell you. I may have needs, of course, because I'm just a newborn but I am *not* needy. I'm a big strong baby. You meet my basic needs and I'll only grow bigger and stronger. I'm also independent. You wait and see. I'll do lots of things on my own."

The dad tells me: "Like father, like son. I ain't the needy type either. Nothin' personal, but it's the kid I care about. I'll be here for as long as he needs me. I'm kinduva 'bad boy.' I smoke cigarettes, which pisses you off. But I'm strong and tough. I know how to do things and how to get places. I guess you could say I'm the capable, efficient type. The kid'll do well because of me. You'll see."

The nursing woman tells me: "Hey, don't worry, Ramona. I don't want to steal your baby or anything. I want you to know I'm your friend. If you find yourself getting worn down, I'm here. I can provide good nourishment for your baby till you feel strong again. Okay? Just know I am here if you need me."

"I" in the dream says: "My! I've given birth to a baby I didn't even know I was expecting. I don't even know if I like this baby. He's cool and self-possessed, not like any other baby I've ever seen. I'll look after him though. Maybe I'll grow to love him. I certainly have lots of mother's milk. Even though I don't like his dad much, I'm glad he wants to look after this child. I won't need to do it all alone."

The woman on the telephone I am not sure about. Perhaps she's a resource within me or represents a useful energy of distraction, keeping macho man out of my face. So how might this translate? Later when I get into rehab over-drive mode - pushing too hard, falling apart, getting down on myself - I have it within me to cry, switch my focus, and slow down. Write, listen to music and rest.

This baby-boy dream is about the new me who needs to learn to walk again. Choosing to adopt this remarkable child's drive, his "Come on, let's go!" attitude, I'll have no problem. He represents a powerful, young, masculine, energetic presence within me. If I nurture myself, that energy will thrive. Yes, give the baby (me) what he needs and he (I) can't be stopped. Fall down? Just get up again. Babies are always learning and learning fast.

This dream reveals to me internal resources/energy supplies I've not been aware of, both yang and yin.

1. Yang: Kick-butt energy supreme - a healthy newborn's vitality and unstoppability.
2. Yang: "Don't mess with me" macho dad energy. The kind that would say, "You get in my way and I'll knock your fuckin' head off!"
3. Yin: Reserve tank energy, deep internal nurturance. Also known as, mommy love.
4. Yin: (implicitly revealed): Well of God energy - comes

from deep inside. Source of my spirituality and creativity? *Yes, God, when I stay connected with you, everything is better.*

The Pesky Young Woman Dream

I'm walking along the street when a pesky young woman catches up to me with a book in her hands. It's a book recently published that I have apparently co-authored with other women. I don't recall ever seeing this book before. What is it about? Nutrition, it looks like. Do I even agree with its contents? It looks helpful. The young woman wants me to autograph her copy. She's persistent and I feel annoyed. She opens the book to the page with all the authors' names and hands me a red ink pen. I notice the names are printed in red. I don't like red ink with red. No contrast. Okay, if that's what she wants. I sign it.

Peskiness Explored

I'm a "semi-expert" on something, perhaps nutrition, and I don't know it. I'm much more knowledgeable than I realize in terms of ways to sustain myself and others. Nutrition is about what people eat and also what they feed on. I don't like my kids or my students feeding on cynicism, for instance, or gratuitously violent books or movies. The pesky young woman recognizes me as "one of the authors." Why a group of authors and why all women?

My perceiving the young woman as pesky suggests she's a shadowy aspect of me I don't like and would prefer to keep hidden. She, this part of me, is trying to get my attention. Well, she's got it now. Time for a little conversation.

"Why are you in my dream? Do you have something you want to tell me?"

"As a matter of fact, yes. I want to tell you which part of you I represent."

"Please do."

"The needy you."

"What?"

"The you that needs to be seen and acknowledged. The you that needs to be differentiated from the rest. More than you want to admit."

"Come on."

"No red upon red for you."

"What do you mean?"

"You like to be noticed, to stand out from the crowd. Think that's a bad thing? Too egotistical or something?"

"Not exactly, but I don't want people to know that about me. I'm an introvert, a private person. I'm a Virgo. You know, the meek, mild, modest type."

"Uh huh."

"What are you smirking about? All right. I do like to be noticed, but only sometimes. And not by splashing."

"Yeah?"

"Listen, smarty pants from my unconscious mind, do you think there's something I want or 'need' to be acknowledged for?"

"Maybe."

"What?"

"For starters, you can acknowledge yourself for remembering this dream, recording it, and then willingly working on it."

"All right, but that's just for me."

"Ramona, I mean it. You need to acknowledge yourself and give yourself credit, not only for this."

"I'm not used to doing that."

"Get used to it."

"What else? Who else do I need to acknowledge me besides me? And for what?"

"It's not my job to tell you the whos or the whats, even if I did know the answers. How about considering the obvious? Maybe you have something 'nutritious' to offer the world. Maybe via the printed word, and maybe with other women."

"Like what?"

"I don't know. You're the one who's got to answer that. It could be something important. Wouldn't that be cool? You 'did' co-author a book. Get this, if I wasn't pesky (your word, by the way), this matter wouldn't even be drawn to your attention. If it wasn't, you might not co-author a book."

"Maybe it's not to be taken literally."

"Or maybe it is. 'Maybe something important'. Ha ha! I guess you

ought to acknowledge me, who's really you, for doing you a favour."
"What favour?"
"Casting sunlight on seeds already planted in your mind."
"What do you mean?"
"You read this dream later and maybe you'll get it."

Wednesday, March 9, 2005, 3:45 p.m.

Good Bye

Melissa came today. I had to say, "I'm sorry. I wish I could handle this song writing assignment but it keeps sucking me back into the wreckage. Could we exchange e-mail addresses and perhaps be in contact later when I'm stronger?"

She said "No." Not appropriate? I felt disappointed. She'd helped me a great deal. I thanked her for everything. I won't see her again.

I'm relieved to say I'm not leaving today. Ray can't come yet, and there's another special brace for me to be fitted with. So Friday it is.

Thursday, March 10, 2005, 7:50 p.m.

Looking Back, Looking Forward

Dear God/Essence, here it is the eve of hospital departure from Richmond and the end of a mini-era. I'm teetering on an edge between past and future. It's a full month since the accident. My body is broken and mending; my nerves are jangled but evening out. My spirits are fluctuating: hopeful and hesitant, determined and scared. Resilient and fragile, I'm like Jingdezhen china.

I survived, without a seatbelt, a head-on collision that should have taken me too. I think of the driver and acknowledge, *God, there but for your grace, go I.* I was extricated, carried and plopped with multiple fractures. For three nights and two and a half days I lay in a Chinese hospital bed. Then Jonathan came.

God, I thank you. I am amazed. It was like a switch flipped and several people's lives were put on hold in order *to help me.*

They responded to a call, scurried and gave their all. Yeming's family, Jonathan, the administrators from HUST, even the men who pulled me from the wreckage for heaven's sake! Not necessarily anything personal; there was something that needed doing.

Who flipped the switch? Did they? Did I? Did you? Or was it all of us collectively, according to "cosmic programming" they and I agreed to before we were born and then forgot? Or perhaps it was nothing of the kind.

Some people believe that souls make promises or agreements for later when they're together on earth, not necessarily based on any karma they owe each other. Maybe Jonathan and I had an agreement. When I consider his initiative, the timing, our cooperation, and the trust we both displayed in going for it, not to mention my safe return to Canada, I am awestruck with the alignment. I am extremely fortunate. I am very blessed. God, for your grace, I again thank you.

The voice I heard in the wreckage, *my* voice, told me my situation was part of a bigger picture involving me and China. I do feel a new direction is in the works. What the bigger picture might be intrigues me, especially my part in it. I wonder if it will involve the vision I created, inspired by Viktor Frankl, about my being back in China and still well connected with Canada. The voice and my vision belong together. I can feel their magnetism.

Dear God, it seems strange to talk to "you" as though you are an entity, a human being, a wise mentor, a friend. Sometimes I wonder how I dare. Given the immensity of all that is - billions-upon-billions of galaxies - your beingness is beyond the scope of any human understanding. I fumble with words that are feeble at best. I call you Essence, but that means nothing. You are what's behind the essence - you created it!

I can't think so big. When I try to, my brain feels like it could explode. It's like you are far away from me, remote. I want to feel your presence. So what do I do? I imagine. I create a personal relationship with you, the powerhouse of all knowing.

Then I flatten my face to the ground at your "feet" and dare to hold a dream in my heart. Because I do, you pick me up and say, "Yes, dare. I need you. I need you to be bold. I need you to need me. I need to feel your power to release my power. You are exalted through me and I am exalted through you. This is how it is." I breathe.

I remember reading words uttered by a wise person about many people being called but few being chosen. God, I humbly say to you, "I feel called. If my choosing to be chosen is your criterion, then with all my heart I say thank you."

It's late. I am present to possibility and to mystery. I shall shut this light off and breathe my way into sleepiness, then slumber. Tomorrow is a new day.

Friday, March 11, 2005, 11:11 a.m.

With Patience and Hard Work

Soon I shall leave the security of these hospital walls. As I await my brother, the wheelchair awaits me. I don't know what's in store. I'm calm and nervous at the same time.

I remember Yeming's good wish message in an e-mail, "*Xin Xiang Shi Cheng*" - What you think in your heart will come true. (With a wish and the swish of a magic wand.)

The *chengyu* Meimei told me about is more in tune with the reality of my needing to learn to walk again. "*Mei Meng Cheng Zhen*" - with patience and hard work, you will realize your beautiful dream. Yes, with this one, the fire burns, the gold's refined, the prize is earned. I shall do my best to stay aligned with my dreams.

Yes, I am ready. The next leg of my journey beckons.

Epilogue

When I first tried to write this last part of my book, I panicked. My head started pounding; then came the vomiting, shaking and weakness. Insomnia complicated matters. These symptoms lasted for two or three days. As hellish as they were, like death throes, I figured I must be in the grip of a good thing, a catharsis. Trauma or tenacious emotional wounding that had been locked in my body for going on eight years was coming out. I could feel it. I'd known all along that writing and publishing my story would be the only way to release the deep shock. The closer I got to publication, the closer I'd be to exposing myself to the world. It was a very frightening thought indeed.

Then a wonderful thing happened. I fell asleep and had a dream. Instinctively I knew it was a healing dream because of how it resonated with my soul. I wrote in my journal:

> *I am in my bedroom, which is also a work area. Beside my computer is a small wax begonia plant in a 6 inch pot. I move it to another place on the desk or onto my dresser but then somehow manage to knock it over. The plant falls on the floor several feet farther than where it should have landed, given the fact that I didn't throw it but only knocked it over. I don't tend to it right away as many people have suddenly arrived in my room, mingling as though at a social function. They seem to be university students or grads. The plant isn't readily noticeable on the dark carpet but luckily no one steps on it or kicks it. When I'm able to take a closer look, I'm surprised to see the pot not just broken but destroyed, beyond any possible salvaging. I'm even more surprised to see the soil and roots still perfectly intact and delicate pink flowers blooming amid tender foliage that suffered no damage. There were no blooms before.*

I feel as though I'm the potted plant. It represents both my book and me. As the pot has been the container for the plant, I have been the container for the trauma. The emotional wounding has simply been there all this time, dormant except for the times I've taken bold action. Those times have included an inner earthquake a few years ago when I purchased a return ticket to China, and more recently, a longer shake-up while I wrote this book.

As for the plant, it produces flowers only after the pot smashes. It's a beautiful surprise that cancels out any distress about its broken container. The pink of the blossoms and the green of the undamaged foliage are colours most pleasing to me. They remind me of the colours of spring, new life and new beginnings.

I did not hurl the plant but the impact of the car accident hurled me and broke my bones. Luckily, I was not beyond salvaging. It's only by my breaking open (like the container) that I can release my story to the world. The story's been in me all this time waiting to be fully formed, crying to be delivered. My book has been breaking me open, similar to the birth of a baby. With my book it's been emotional pain. With childbirth it's physical pain. In both instances, creation triumphs over pain.

This dream is touching me so deeply I can hardly believe it. The baby is my story of love for China. The trauma is only one part of this bigger, more beautiful story. In the wreckage I heard, "I don't know what this is all about but I do know it's part of a bigger picture and it's a good picture and it involves me and China." With all my heart all these years I have wanted to tell my story and now I am finally doing it. This is a healing dream. How could I be anything but thankful?

Now to breathe. The processing goes on and on. Two more books call to be written. The first is what happened before my first trip to China and the second is what happened afterwards. Many people have asked why I ventured to a foreign land and left behind my good life in Canada. They've asked how I prepared for such a shift and what it was like to live and teach in northern China. That book is mostly written. My return to China could be a sequel. I don't know if my story will ever be over. There is unfolding and unfolding, like the petals of a blossoming flower.

The *I Ching* says that completion is actually transition. New beginnings are implicit in endings. I am living my destiny.

Glossary of Chinese Terms

Bai Qiu En - Dr. Norman Bethune, Canadian surgeon viewed as a hero in China

Bu Liao Qing - "Love Without End," a song made famous by actress Lin Dai in a Chinese classic film

bu si niao - immortal bird, used in reference to the phoenix

Chang'e - Chinese mortal turned goddess, living on the moon

Chang'e xia fan - used to describe a girl's beauty: Chang'e has returned to earth

chengyu - four character idiom, often derived from classical Chinese literature

da jiang shan rong yi, zuo jiang shan nan - to conquer a country is easy; to govern it well is hard

da nan bu si, bi you hou fu - literally big bad thing don't die, then have good fortune; if you survive a disaster, you are guaranteed great fortune and happiness

Ding Xiang Hua - "Lilac," a sad song about a girl named for the flower

dong tian guo qu le - literally winter has passed; hardships are over

erhu - traditional two-stringed Chinese instrument, sometimes referred to as the Chinese violin fenghuang - phoenix

fenghuang shu - phoenix tree

feng yu guo hou shi cai hong - after wind and rain is a rainbow, hard times will pass and things will be much better

guaiguaide - be good

Guanyin - Buddhist goddess of mercy

Gulangyu - a tiny island near Xiamen in Fujian province, sometimes referred to as the "Island of Pianos"

haojile - wonderful

hongbao - literally red envelope; at Spring Festival children receive these with money tucked inside

hua long dian jing - literally paint dragon, dot eyes; a chengyu meaning to add the finishing touches to something and have it come to life in a remarkable way

I Ching – ancient Chinese text consulted for guidance

jiao hua – sly teacher

ke ai de - cute, lovely, sweet

ku nan de ren sheng zhi hui shi yi zhi jian qiang de ren geng qiang da - a hard life will only make a strong-spirited person stronger

Lao Shu Ai Da Mi - "Mice Love (or A Mouse Loves) Rice," a cute Chinese pop song

liang shi yi you - a chengyu meaning you are my good teacher, my mentor and my dear friend

long - dragon

long feng cheng xiang - literally dragon phoenix become successful, a chengyu meaning the dragon and the phoenix together bring good fortune

Lu Xun - renowned writer and satirist of the 20th Century

mei lan zhu ju - literally plum, orchid, bamboo, chrysanthemum; a chengyu honouring these special plants (referred to as the "Four Gentlemen") for their qualities

mei meng cheng zhen - literally beautiful dream becomes real, a chengyu meaning a beautiful dream that is hard to realize will come true if you are patient and industrious

meng li - in my dreams

mo li hua - jasmine flower

ni chi le ma? - have you eaten?

ni hao - literally you good; hello.

ni hen hao - you are very good/kind/nice

pinyin - uses the same alphabet as Western languages to approximate Chinese sounds; all the Chinese words in this list are shown in pinyin

qiang da chu tou niao - an idiom meaning the bird that sticks its head out of the nest will have his head shot off; in other words, do not stand out if you want to be safe

shou de yun kai jian yue ming - literally wait for the clouds to open, see the moon bright; keep your faith alive and things will get better

Shou Xing - literally star of human life, Taoist god of longevity

Tao - way the universe works, essence of the Universe that keeps everything functional and in balance, sometimes referred to as the way

tao guang yang hui - literally hide light nourish weaknesses, a chengyu meaning to hide your talents as you develop your character

tao yan - something like you're disgusting or I hate you; often used by a girl to feign dislike for a boy who's interested in her

wai jiao - foreign teacher

wang nian zhi jiao - literally forget year (age) friendship, the friendship of forgetting age difference

wei wu wei - a Taoist concept: do without doing

wo ai ni men - I love you guys

wo bao le - I'm full

wo shi Jianadaren - I'm Canadian

xiang - think

xiao - little

xie xie ni - thank you so much

xin nian kuaile - Happy New Year

xin xiang shi cheng - literally heart thinking becomes successful, a chengyu meaning the dreams in your heart will be realized

xi xin - literally wash heart

zhe ge - this/these ones

zou ba - let's go

Book Club Discussion Questions

1. "You can't judge a book by its cover." Or can you? Discuss both cover and title and how they relate to the book.

2. The concepts of fate and destiny come up a number of times both directly and indirectly. (Notably page 60.) Are they the same? Was the accident fate and/or part of the author's destiny or neither?

3. In the prologue and later, Ramona writes about receiving and following "the guidance of a still small voice." Have you experienced anything similar? If yes, was being in a state of duress a necessary component? How has paying attention to the voice, or not, affected your life?

4. On page 16, Ramona refers to the "language of the heart" as being different from the language of explanations. What do you think she means by this? Are there any passages that "speak to your heart"?

5. A photo of a rock with "xi xin" (wash your heart) appears at the front of the story, seeming to indicate its importance in the mind of the author. Later on (page 140-141), she shares her thoughts about "wash your heart." Does this seem to you to be the story's main message? If not, what do you think is?

6. What differences and similarities between your way of life and that of the people in this story did you notice? Did any surprise you?

7. Many people in the West/ "First World" only know about China through mainstream media. From what you know about

China, what problems do the people there face? Are we affected by those problems at all? Do we contribute to some of them?

8. Eria, Haiwu and Yeming were 22 years old when this story took place. As members of a transitional generation in China, what role might they have in the "new China"? What is the "new China"? What are your predictions about China?

9. Dancing in the Heart of the Dragon is largely a story of friendship, both cross-cultural and cross-generational. How common are these types of friendship in your society? What are the benefits?

10. Ramona shares and interprets nine dreams. Are they a distraction or do they add depth to her story? Have you ever remembered your dreams, written them down and worked with them? If so, was doing so a worthwhile experience?

11. Who was your favourite character? What did you appreciate about him/her?

12. Share passages that stood out for you. What made them stand out? Did you feel with any of them that you were "right there" with the author? If so, how was she able to "bring you along"?

13. The author decided to start her story in an airport washroom then continue from a hospital bed, switching back and forth in time. Did this kind of structure work for you? Was sharing the accident early on a good idea? What did you think of the story's being told through narrative, journal entries, email correspondence, and conversations?

14. If Dancing in the Heart of the Dragon were made into a movie, how would you recommend it be filmed? Who would you cast in the roles? What about a soundtrack?

15. Has this book caused you to rethink any of your previously held opinions? Do you think it's important for Westerners to learn about China? How might the West and China learn from each other?

Author Biography

Born in Vancouver, Canada, the eldest of six, Ramona grew up with a dream to "go to a foreign land one day and live there." After earning a BA in English from UBC, she started her teaching career in Port McNeill, B.C., then took time off to raise three children. Later she returned to teaching in Nanaimo, B.C. and also earned her MA in educational leadership. In early 2004, disenchanted with just about everything, Ramona responded to an inner voice telling her she was "going to China," a decision central to a purpose she was meant to fulfill and a decision she has not regretted. Ramona now lives in Victoria, BC, with her grandchildren nearby. Writing continues to be a main source of her spiritual connection. This is her first book.

For more information please visit www.RamonaMckean.com

or

Contact the author at ramona.mckean@gmail.com

If you want to get on the path to be a published author by **Influence Publishing** please go to **www.InspireABook.com**

Inspiring books that influence change

More information on our other titles and how to submit your own proposal can be found at **www.InfluencePublishing.com**

CPSIA information can be obtained at www.ICGtesting.com
Printed in the USA
LVOW060852100713

342097LV00002B/12/P